Joseph Butler, Thomas B. Kilpatrick

Sermons I, II, III

Upon Human Nature or Man Considered as a Moral Agent

Joseph Butler, Thomas B. Kilpatrick

Sermons I, II, III
Upon Human Nature or Man Considered as a Moral Agent

ISBN/EAN: 9783337087326

Printed in Europe, USA, Canada, Australia, Japan

Cover: Foto ©Lupo / pixelio.de

More available books at **www.hansebooks.com**

SERMONS

BY THE RIGHT REVEREND FATHER IN GOD

JOSEPH BUTLER, D.C.L.,

LATE LORD BISHOP OF DURHAM.

SERMONS I., II., III.

UPON HUMAN NATURE, OR MAN CONSIDERED AS A MORAL AGENT.

Introduction and Notes

BY THE

REV. THOMAS B. KILPATRICK, B.D.,

MINISTER AT FERRYHILL, ABERDEEN.

PREFACE.

THE aim of this little book is twofold. In the first place, an effort is made so to explain and illustrate Butler's Three Sermons on Human Nature that they shall be made intelligible and attractive to readers who may feel themselves repelled by a style which is at times obscure and unpleasant. In the second place, the hope is entertained of engaging and directing in a course of ethical study some who may not yet have seriously considered the interest and importance of such a pursuit. No attempt is made to be exhaustive or even systematic. The aim of the book will be amply realized, if readers have their interest in the subject of ethics awakened, and arise to make for themselves a more competent and satisfactory study.

It may be objected that ethical study is far too abstruse and difficult for those whom the editors chiefly have in view in issuing their series of Bible Class Handbooks. The difficulty may be granted; and to those who believe that no good thing can be got without effort, the difficulty of the subject will be no reason against its being taught to all who are gifted with ordinary intelligence, even though they may not have received a scientific training. The charge of want of interest or of remoteness from practical life must be earnestly repudiated. What can lie nearer to our interest, what can be more profitable for all who seek nobility of life, than the study of those principles which mould the character and determine the conduct? If ever there was a time when ethical study was needed, not only among the cultured few, but among the unphilosophic multitude, it is now. Social life is becoming more complex, its problems deeper and more hard of solution. Political life is wider, and political responsibilities rest upon well-nigh every individual in the state, however poor or ill-educated. Never was there a time when moral fallacies spread so swiftly, or were fraught with more disastrous consequences. If the democracy is to rule in righteousness, it must be educated in true notions of what right is. The young men and maidens who pass through clerical hands for instruction hold in their power the moral destinies of the empire. Most needful is it, therefore, that pains be taken to aid them to think clearly and truly on moral subjects, so that their decisions on the moral problems presented to them in their individual, social, or political life, should be clear, definite, and true. It may be objected, further, that such a study is at least non-religious. Many good men object to it as placing too high a value on "mere morality." It is rather hard to have to meet such an objection. It ought not to be necessary to refer such objectors to the New Testament, that they may see for themselves the place which ethical teaching holds there. There is a Sermon on the Mount, there are maxims and parables, surely enough to prove the value our Lord puts upon morality. The Epistles in like manner abound in special and careful treatment bestowed on moral subjects. Nothing is more striking than the zest with which the Apostle Paul rises from the highly doctrinal to the intensely practical, and his evident anxiety that no doctrine shall seem to hang in the air merely, without firm footing on the plane of actual life and conduct. Let the proportions of the New Testament be observed, and ethical study has nothing to fear in the way of being undervalued or restricted. Besides, if there be a truth at all in this sneer at "mere morality," it is one which no Christian moralist has ever overlooked. It has been often observed, and in this little book it shall be specially emphasized, that the true basis of ethics is religion. Morality, falsely abstracted and held apart from religion, is indeed "mere morality," mere failure. Morality, having its springs in religion, looking to religion for its crown and consummation, is the interpretation of religion, its translation into terms of daily life, its fullest vindication, its noblest apologetic. Let those who hastily condemn writing or preaching as being merely moral beware of what they are doing. There is no deadlier heresy than the separation of religion and morality. Language, therefore, which would even suggest that they were separable is most dangerous, and imperils the whole truth of the Gospel. These things ought ye to have done, and not to have left the other undone. Were religious writings and evangelical sermons to contain more ethical teaching than they commonly do, it would not make them the less religious and evangelical, and it would make them far more adequate to scriptural and divine truth, and would bring them into far closer connection with the needs of man. With the aim, then, of reviving and spreading abroad among the people an interest in ethical study, several methods might be adopted. A handbook might be prepared which would deal with the whole range of ethics, and give at least the outline of a system. A most useful textbook would be one which should confine itself strictly to New Testament ethics, and examine the various moral ideas to be found in the teaching of Christ, and in other parts of the New Testament. The method adopted by the editors has been to take an English author whose views are contained in brief compass, and make him a door of entrance, as it were, into the subject. The author they have chosen is Joseph Butler, whose sermons on Human Nature contain the gist of his teaching. In using this author in this way, several things naturally occur as necessary to be done. It will be necessary to recall the main features of the man's life; for as a man lives, so will his thinking be. It will be requisite also to note his place in the history of thought, and to see whom he succeeded and by whom he was surrounded in this department of study. A compendious statement of his views will be useful ; as also an estimate of them in the light of later developments. These things are attempted in the Introduction. The Notes form a kind of commentary. They try to explain the author's meaning where that seems obscure. They offer a few illustrations and examples from literature of ideas occurring in the text. In some cases also they take up suggestions and seek to develop them constructively. It has not been possible to avoid altogether technicalities in language, or turns of thought more familiar to the student than to the general reader. Where such difficulties belong not to the subject but to its treatment, the notes are of course faulty, and of their deficiency in this and manifold other respects the writer is keenly aware. It is hoped, however, that with all its defects, this little book may be helpful in deepening in the minds of others an interest which the writer has profoundly at heart.

T. B. K.

ABERDEEN, *1st May* 1888.

CONTENTS.

———o———

	PAGE
INTRODUCTION,	11–50
§ 1. Biographical Sketch,	11–15
§ 2. The Aim and Value of Ethical Study,	15–20
§ 3. The Rise of Modern (British) Ethical Study : Thomas Hobbes,	20–23
§ 4. Answers to Hobbes : Shaftesbury and Hutcheson,	24–26
§ 5. Butler's Ethical Doctrine : Standpoint and Method,	26–30
§ 6. Butler's Ethical Doctrine : Statement,	30–37
§ 7. Butler's Ethical Doctrine : Estimate,	37–43
§ 8. Concluding Remarks,	43–50
TEXT AND NOTES,	51–123

INTRODUCTION.

---o---

§ 1. BIOGRAPHICAL SKETCH.

THE incidents of Butler's life are very few, and may be told very briefly. The future bishop was the son of a shopkeeper, and was born at Wantage, in Berkshire, in the year 1692. His father, who was a Presbyterian, destined him for the ministry; and, after a few years spent in the grammar school, he was sent to a Nonconformist academy, then situated in Gloucester, but soon after removed to Tewkesbury. Here he remained till past his twenty-second year. The only remarkable feature of his career so far is the correspondence which took place between him and Dr. Clarke, the author of *A Demonstration of the Being and Attributes of God*, which was published in 1704. The criticisms which Butler then offered on Clarke's work he afterwards withdrew; but his having ventured to make them at all shows the meditative cast of his mind displaying itself thus early. About this time he determined to abandon the non-conformity in which he had been reared, and to conform to the Established Church of England. We might be disposed, in view of the worldly success which afterwards befell him, to question the purity of his motives in taking this step. In his whole life, however, we see only deep quietude and even lethargy of spirit, to which active self-seeking and restless ambition were utterly uncongenial. We shall find the true explanation to lie, on the one hand, in the decadent spirituality of the Nonconformist bodies of the time, which rendered them incapable of commanding the enthusiastic loyalty even of their own members; and, on the other, in the tone and temper of Butler's mind, which, at once meditative and devout, found itself attracted by the ceremonial worship of Episcopacy, and the mystical theology often, though by no means always or necessarily, characteristic of it. It is interesting to note that Thomas Secker, a school companion of Butler's, and his life-long friend, made the same transition, and ultimately attained the highest position the Church could afford, the Archbishopric of Canterbury. In 1714, Butler entered Oxford as a student of Oriel College, and in 1717 received ordination. At Oxford he made a friendship to which he was afterwards indebted for promotion, that of Edward Talbot, whose father was then Bishop of Salisbury, and afterwards Bishop of Durham. Through this powerful influence he was appointed preacher at the Rolls Chapel in 1718; rector of Haughton-le-Skerne, near Darlington, in 1722; and, in 1725, rector of Stanhope, a benefice so rich that it obtained the name of the "golden rectory." In the following year he resigned his post as preacher at the Rolls Chapel, and published fifteen of the sermons which he had preached during his tenure of office. Most of these directly develop his ethical theory, as their titles indicate: "Upon Human Nature, or man considered as a Moral Agent" (i., ii., iii.), "Upon Compassion" (v., vi.), "Upon Resentment and Forgiveness of Injuries" (viii., ix.), "Upon the Love of our Neighbour" (xi., xii.). Others are more incidental in their character: "Upon the Government of the Tongue" (iv.), "Upon the Character of Balaam" (vii.), "Upon Self-Deceit" (x.), "Upon the Ignorance of Man" (xv.). Two are of unique interest and special importance for a full study of his thought: "Upon Piety, or the Love of God" (xiii., xiv.). In no sense do these sermons constitute a system. His views are there, but in disjointed, sermonic form; a fact which doubtless helped to disguise from the author himself their occasional mutual inconsistencies. His own remark in concluding the preface is: "It may be proper first to advertise the reader, that he is not to look for any particular reason for the choice of the greatest part of these discourses; their being taken from amongst many others, preached in the same place, through a course of eight years, being in great measure accidental. Neither is he to expect to find any other connection between them than that uniformity of thought and design which will always be found in the writings of the same person, when he writes with simplicity and in earnest." Whatever may be said of the literary merit of these sermons, the style of which is often obscure through too great compression, or of the value of their ethical theory, which may afford grounds for criticism, the "simplicity" of the author's motive and the "earnestness" of his purpose are sufficiently obvious, and are worthy of truest respect and admiration. One would like to know if the services were well attended, and if any of the audience, who may have come through custom or curiosity, left with the throb of rising nobility of purpose beating in their bosoms. For six years he remained at Stanhope immersed in the train of thought which issued in the famous *Analogy*. Queen Caroline, who had heard of him from his old friend Secker, and had been surprised to learn that he was still living, remarked on another occasion to a Church dignitary that she had imagined Mr. Butler was dead. "No, madam," was the reply, "he is not dead, but he is buried." The resurrection very speedily took place. He was made chaplain to the Lord Chancellor; and on his way to London he visited Oxford, where he received the degree of Doctor of Law. This period seems to have been more full of living interest than any other in his uneventful life. In 1736 he received a prebend in the church of Rochester. In the same year he was made Clerk of the Closet, and became a regularly invited guest at those supper parties at which Queen Caroline assembled the leading divines of the day and listened with interest, and we may hope with intelligence, to their discussions upon theological subjects. In this year also he published his *Analogy of Religion, Natural and Revealed, to the Constitution and Course of Nature*, a work which has, perhaps too exclusively, guided the lines along which the defence of Christian truth has proceeded down to the present day, and the fame of which has somewhat cast into the shade the real value of the sermons. With this year Butler's literary history ends. In 1738 he was made a bishop, and amid the cares of such an office he probably lacked the leisure, and perhaps even lost the capacity, for fresh literary effort. His first see was Bristol, which he held for eleven years. In 1750 he was translated to Durham. The first and only charge which he addressed to his clergy attracted considerable attention, and provoked some hostility by expressions which to the unsophisticated minds of the day savoured of a tendency towards Roman superstitions. For two years he continued to discharge the duties and dispense the charities of his magnificent but most onerous position. His health, however, gave way under the strain, and he died at Bath, June 16, 1752. His last thoughts seem to have gathered round his boyhood's friend Secker, who was then Bishop of Oxford. He was buried in his old cathedral of Bristol. After his death an attempt was made to revive the charge of Romanism which had been brought against him during his life. It was even asserted that he had died in the communion of the Church of Rome. These suspicions were finally disposed of through the testimony of Secker, now Archbishop of Canterbury, who thus rendered a last service to the friend whose career had been so strangely parallel to his own.

A man's thought, if it be true and genuine, is the expression of his character, from which it derives its distinctive peculiarities. Between Butler's ethical theory, accordingly, and his life there is an obvious and striking resemblance. He stands in marked contrast to the men among whom he lived and worked. He is pure in his own practice; quiet, reflective, unenergetic in his disposition; absorbed in studies of human nature, brooding over questions of right and duty. Around him seethes a world of scheme, and ambition, and intrigue, which knows no higher standard than temporal benefit, and no loftier motive than selfishness more or less disguised. In like manner, his moral teaching is directly opposed to the prevailing conceptions of the day. It vindicates the claim of duty against theories which laboured to elevate to the rank of a speculative truth and a practical guide the demand of self to be supreme and uncontrolled. It is remarkable that the world made no attempt to persecute the man whose words, illustrated as these were by his personal character, so fully condemned it. It was stirred to no resentment, and heaped its highest honours on one whom it recognised to be wholly unlike itself. Bagehot's explanation of the phenomenon is given with his usual keenness of expression: "We may admire what we cannot share; reverence what we do not imitate. At any rate, so thought the contemporaries of Butler. They did, as a Frenchman would say, 'their possible' for a good man; at least they made him a bishop" (*Literary Studies*, vol. ii. p. 60). It is less remarkable that Butler did not perceive the full extent of his difference from prevailing views on moral subjects. It has often happened that a thinker has missed the central position of his own thought; and while preparing the way for further developments, has not himself perceived the full consequences of his own teaching.

§ 2. THE AIM AND VALUE OF ETHICAL STUDY.

There are three great relationships in which, as human beings, we stand, toward nature, toward our fellow-men, and toward God. In these, broadly speaking, our lives are spent, and through these our natures are developed on their various sides, physical, moral, and spiritual. We may live in these spheres of being, and occupy ourselves abundantly in their activities, and become through such exercise strong in physical frame, sound in moral constitution, reverent and devout in soul, long before the reflective faculty fully awakes and prompts us to ask definitely what is the nature and value of the life we have been living so busily, and what is the source and truth of the principles whose validity we have taken for granted, while we unquestioningly guided our conduct by them. Life necessarily precedes thought; and it is, of course, possible to live almost without thought. Some are found, also, who make a boast of living without troubling themselves as to any questions which lie beyond the range of their immediate practical concerns, and deliberately undervalue the importance of natural science, or moral philosophy, or theology. It is obvious, however, that this is to be untrue to our constitution as rational beings, endowed with the faculty of reflection, and possessed of the thirst for truth, which, however much it may be ignored for the sake of mere material concerns, cannot be wholly quenched. It will be found, too, that those who deny the importance of thought in name of the supreme interest of life, in the end fail to do justice to that very life in which they absorb themselves to the exclusion of all interest in the work of thought. The work of thought, accordingly, is to investigate the relationships in which we stand, and through our place in which we are what we are; to discover the principles which bear sway in the different departments of our life; and to perceive how, by their means, our fragmentary and incidental experiences are woven into the completeness of perfect and well-developed manhood. (1) We live in the world of nature. It shines upon us in its loveliness. It awes us with its might. It ministers to us out of its abundance. Upon the vast multitude of details thus presented to our observation, thought proceeds to operate, discerning the laws and principles that are at work amid all these various elements, and thus out of the chaos of isolated facts constructing a realm of order and harmony. The result of this work of thought is to show us nature, not as an alien power to which we must submit as an irrational fact, but as itself the product and manifestation of that which constitutes our own being, viz. mind or spirit. The special sciences are each labouring at some particular department of this mighty task; while it is the work of philosophy or metaphysics to examine the principles and methods of each science, to compare the conclusions of all, and to reach a standpoint higher than that which is possible to any one of them. Thought, therefore, sets us free in the presence of nature, enables us to adjust the methods of our life to the great laws that govern the material universe, and sometimes even to subdue to our own ends the mighty forces which are there at work. (2) We live in the world of human fellowship. This world touches us yet more nearly than that of nature. That was always in some sense beyond us. But of this we are ourselves essential parts. We are members of families. We belong to social communities, larger or smaller. We are citizens of the State. In all these capacities our private life is bound up with that of our fellows. Every deed of ours, however personal, has its issues in the surrounding social sphere; while nothing takes place there which does not in some shape or form modify our condition or direct our conduct. No man, how much soever he may desire to seclude himself from the world, can live and act at all without influencing for weal or woe some other human being, and without in turn being influenced by persons whom, it may be, he never saw, or by actions in which he bore no individual part. The social fabric to which we belong is built up, accordingly, out of innumerable parts, whose combination and interdependence is of the most complex and delicate description. One shudders to think how easily chaos and disorder might penetrate into the sphere of our social life, and sink it lower than that of the brutes, which, amid all their savagery and unreason, acknowledge the constraint of certain natural ties. The Reign of Terror during the French Revolution, or the condition of some parts of Ireland in our own day, show what terrible results may follow from ignorance of the constitution of the moral world, and defiance of the fundamental principles which should regulate the relations of man to man. Here, therefore, lies the task of thought, which has to perform for the world of human relationships what it does for the world of nature. It has to inquire how the social fabric has been erected, what laws and principles underlie its endless variety, and by what means it may be maintained in permanence and integrity. The determination of points like these is, at the same time, the discovery for the individual of those facts and laws by the recognition and observance of which his own moral character is developed and his own highest good attained. He finds that the moral world, like the world of nature, is not an alien sphere where he has to fight for his independent existence, with the perpetual chance of sinking in the struggle, but is the revelation of that which constitutes his own true being, affording for him, therefore, a home in which, through obedience to the laws which obtain there, he may attain the full freedom and joy of life. This division of the work of thought, accordingly, is committed to moral philosophy or ethics. The latter term is derived from ἦθος, "character;" and we may accept the definition of this study as "the doctrine of character." We must remember, however, that the character of the individual cannot be described by reference to himself alone. We must always take into consideration the society of which he forms a part. There is no true moral excellence for man in isolation from his fellows. The principles by loyal adherence to which he reaches the perfection of his own being are those which are creative of the moral organism in which he lives and moves and has his being. To discern these principles, to exhibit the extent of their application, to vindicate their authority and function as at once the law of duty for the individual and the means of his attaining the highest excellence of which he is capable, is the aim of ethical study. (3) We live in the world of God's grace. We are the objects of a purpose of mercy, operative amid the daily beneficences of food and raiment and comfort, amid the discipline and teaching of our experience of life, and amid higher and more direct influences that touch our souls. To comprehend that purpose, to trace its historical unfolding from first dawn of promise to fulfilment in the crowning deed of infinite Love, and to grasp, however imperfectly, its issues in world-wide victory and personal holiness, is the task of theology. Here the energy of thought reaches the highest exercise of which it is capable under the conditions in which we "know in part." The moral sphere, accordingly, holds a middle position. On the one hand is the world of physical nature, which enters into the moral sphere, in so far as it presents a field for the development of many of the qualities which go to form the completeness of moral character. On the other hand is the realm of grace, within which the moral sphere is itself comprehended, and from which it derives the ultimate interpretation and vindication of its principles. In other words, we may say that morality includes within the scope of its influence and judgment the physical activities of man, giving to them dignity and worth, and estimating them by moral standards; while it is itself included in religion, and derives from it its highest conceptions of right and its mightiest impulses of action. In pursuing the study of ethics, therefore, we must admit and recognise the work of thought in other departments, and must be ready to harmonize the results to which we are led in the moral sphere with those established by the natural sciences on the one side and theology on the other. At the same time, it is perfectly possible, and for purposes of method necessary, to leave science and theology without much explicit reference to them, and to fix the attention upon the moral sphere alone, making a special and in part separate study of ethics.

The value of such a study is apparent when we realize its aim. We are accustomed to say that "knowledge is power;" and we illustrate this remark by pointing to the wonderful achievements of science by which man has been enabled to overcome the most stupendous physical obstacles, and well-nigh annihilate space and time. The same remark applies to the moral sphere. Every endeavour which sets before us the constitution of the moral world, and makes plain to us the principles on which it is framed, and by which our moral nature grows, will aid us to live more worthily in it. It is not meant that a talented and learned man is necessarily a better man than one less highly endowed or less advantageously situated, or that in difficult and perplexing circumstances he will act more conformably to right and duty. It is true, however, that all men, as moral and responsible agents, are required to face all the moral facts of life, and to seek, by every effort of mind and soul, to solve the moral problems which present themselves on every hand. Ignorance of facts which is produced by ignoring them, incapacity to solve problems which is begotten of unwillingness to face them, are moral faults, and tend to lower the moral tone of a community which may be otherwise fairly cultured, and will blunt the conscience and degrade the practice of individuals who may be competent men of science, or, painful as it is to contemplate, trained theologians. The maintenance of a high standard of public opinion, the moral elevation of the community, the perfecting of individual rectitude, cannot be entrusted to intentions, instincts, feelings. Knowledge is required; and the community, or Church, or individual which wilfully declines its acquisition, will assuredly pay the penalty of moral deterioration. Medical men tell us that much of the misery and disease which exist among certain *strata* of society is due to the ignorance which prevails there as to the elemental facts regarding health. Medical science, therefore, is devoting itself more and more to teaching the fundamental rules of physical wellbeing. We may add that much of the inconsistency too often remarked among those men who make a high Christian profession, and many of the sad lapses into immorality or crime, are due to the prevailing habit of ignoring the elemental facts regarding righteousness. It is awfully possible to be acquainted with the doctrines of grace, and even to have passed through various phases of religious experience, without having grasped the fundamental distinctions of right and wrong, and without exhibiting so high a moral tone, as those who it may be never heard of those doctrines or passed through these experiences. Let it be understood that we are citizens of the moral world; and let it be realized that to live worthily in it we must know it. Patient study of the facts to be observed amid the complex phenomena of social life will make keen our perception of moral distinctions, will make clear and definite the utterances of conscience, and will give added force to our pursuit of righteousness. In this broad sense it is true, according to the ancient saying, that "virtue is knowledge." To live well requires an effort of thought, from the obligation of which we cannot escape by any amount of fine feeling. Moral philosophy, of course, will not produce moral men. Though this be true, however, the value of ethical study in clearing our thoughts and deepening our convictions on moral questions is neither remote nor small.

§ 3. THE RISE OF MODERN BRITISH ETHICAL STUDY: THOMAS HOBBES.

Throughout the period of the Middle Ages, every department of thought and life lay in strict subjection to the authority of the Church. At the Reformation this despotism was destroyed, and men were forced to seek a surer ground of truth, and a mightier impulse for action, than the mere dictates of an outward power. In the spiritual sphere, a human priesthood, wielding the instruments of a cumbrous and enslaving ritual, had long stood between the soul and God. Now, men learned to seek in personal fellowship with Christ Himself the reconciliation with God which was their deepest need. The great principle of the Reformation, expressed in the doctrine of justification by faith, is simply the rest of the human spirit upon God as He is revealed in Christ. From Christ alone, without any human mediation, there is obtained that freedom from condemnation, and that power for righteousness, in which spiritual life truly consists. In the intellectual sphere, the only material upon which human thought had for centuries been allowed to exercise itself consisted of the dogmas of the Church; and the only method it was permitted to employ was the logic of Aristotle. Now, however, we find Descartes pushing his way through doubt after doubt, till he reaches the certainty of self-consciousness, and finds there the basis both of being and of thought; and we find Bacon directing men to look to experience for the source of truth, and thus inaugurating that development of physical science of which our century has seen such marvellous issues. In the moral sphere the same process repeats itself. The Church theologians elaborated a body of laws for the regulation of conduct. The administration and application of these was the work of priests in the confessional, as so-called directors of the conscience. Morality was identified with submission to the laws thus framed and administered. Ethical study, therefore, resolved itself into casuistry, or the discussion, illustration, and manipulation of these laws, with the practical result of wholly befogging the conscience and providing justification for any conduct, however defiant of truth and righteousness. It was inevitable, therefore, that, when in this department also the despotism of an external authority was discarded, men should seek for a reliable ground of moral conduct, a trustworthy standard of action, an adequate source of righteous impulse. The man with whom, in England, this line of inquiry originated was Thomas Hobbes (born at Malmesbury 1588, died at Hardwick 1679). It is impossible to understand the subsequent course of British ethical study, and in particular the place which Butler holds as a writer on ethical subjects, without noting, at least in outline, the results reached by Hobbes. His views seemed to suit the society of his day, whose opinions and practice they largely influenced. His method was employed even by those who disagreed with him. His conclusions, even when they were not accepted, formed the starting-point of further discussion, and thus originated the very theories in which they were contradicted and opposed. Briefly, then, the two essential points of his theory are his doctrine of human nature and his doctrine of society. (1) Man's primary condition is that of appetite, sense of want, or desire. His first endeavour is to satisfy his needs and gratify his desires. All man's natural tendencies, therefore, are "self-regarding." Hobbes wavers a little as to the end which man naturally seeks, making it sometimes pleasure and sometimes mere self-preservation. In any case, his position is that man naturally seeks and can seek only selfish ends. The Right of Nature (Jus Naturale) "is the liberty each man hath to use his own power as he will himself for the preservation of his own nature, that is to say, of his own life." The state of nature, accordingly, is that condition of affairs in which every man seeks his own individual satisfaction, irrespective of the needs of his fellow-men. The inevitable consequence is universal strife. The state of nature in complete form and universal prevalence is prehistoric; but in scarcely diminished form we see it among savages, or in the relation of the European Powers; and we find traces of it even in civilised society. Hobbes brings out with great power the miseries attendant on such a mode of existence. "In such a condition there is no place for industry, because the fruit thereof is uncertain, and consequently no culture of the earth, no navigation nor use of the commodities that may be imported by sea, no commodious building, no instruments of moving and removing such things as require much force, no knowledge of the face of the earth, no account of time, no arts, no letters, no society, and, which is worst of all, continual fear and danger of violent death, and the life of man, solitary, poor, nasty, brutish, and short. . . It is consequent also to the same conditions that there be no propriety, no dominion, no *mine* and *thine* distinct, but only that to be every man's that he can get and for so long as he can keep it." (2) This state of matters, of course, proves unsupportable; and man, aiming as he does and can only do at self-satisfaction, casts about forthwith for means of emergence from it. His nature prompts him to seek pleasure, or, at least, self-preservation. Reason is the faculty by which he is enabled to devise the means best calculated to procure the ends to which his nature impels him. This calculating faculty, accordingly, prescribes to him, as on the whole the best means of attaining his ends as an individual, deference to the wishes and desires of the many. Man, therefore, has no natural affection for his fellows. His "social affections" are the original "self-regarding" affections, taught by bitter experience to see that the attainment of their own ends requires the furtherance of the interests of others. "Because the condition of man is a condition of war of every one against every one . . . it followeth, that in such a condition, every man has a right to everything, even to one another's body. And, therefore, as long as this natural right of every man to everything endureth, there can be no security to any man (how strong and wise soever he be) of living out the time which nature ordinarily alloweth men to live. And consequently it is a precept or general rule of Reason, That every man ought to endeavour Peace. . . . From this . . . is derived this second law, That a man be willing, when others are so too, as far forth as for peace and defence of himself he shall think it necessary, to lay down his right to all things, and be contented with so much liberty against other men as he would allow other men against himself." Reason, however, has in itself no power to create such social conditions as shall make it profitable for men thus to practise mutual forbearance. The only guarantee for the maintenance of such a state is a strong government, by the terror of whose power the natural passions, which reason alone is too weak to control, may be kept in strict subjection. It is necessary, therefore, for the individuals of which society is composed "to confer all their power and strength upon one Man or Assembly of Men, that may reduce all their wills, by plurality of Voices, unto one Will." There must be, of course, entire reciprocity in this surrender of right. Each man must in effect say to his fellow, " I authorize and give up my right of governing myself to this Man, or to this Assembly of Men, on this condition, that thou give up thy right to him, and authorize all his actions in like manner." Thus by mutual consent there is generated " that great leviathan, that mortal god, to which we owe under the immortal God our power and defence." It matters not whether the force of government be monarchical or republican, if only it possess the indispensable requisite. Men are free not to erect this power over themselves; but once it is erected, the first duty of man is submission, the most heinous of crimes is rebellion. Hobbes illustrated this doctrine throughout his life in a way which, if not quite honourable, was at least logically consistent. Under Charles I. he maintained a high doctrine of absolute monarchy. When the government of Cromwell seemed likely to be permanent, he made his peace with it. And when the Restoration took place, he reverted without difficulty to his monarchical views.

§ 4. ANSWERS TO HOBBES: SHAFTESBURY AND HUTCHESON.

The views of Hobbes were so startling, and in many respects so repellent, that students of ethics felt themselves bound to prepare replies to his conclusions, and to establish a theory which might be more in harmony with the instincts of humanity. Among those who devoted themselves to this purpose the most important is Lord Shaftesbury (1671–1713). His works were published in 1711 under the title of *Characteristics of Men, Manners, Opinions, Times*. The second volume contains his chief ethical treatise, the *Enquiry concerning Virtue and Merit*. It is important to notice that his method is almost identically that of Hobbes. Instead of coming down upon Hobbes out of some heavenly region of abstract thought, Shaftesbury and his followers invaded the realm where Hobbes had proclaimed himself master, and undertook his defeat with his own weapons. He had devoted himself to the study of human nature; so would they, but with greater minuteness. He had employed that method of observation which Bacon had bequeathed to his countrymen as the instrument of research in respect both of things material and things spiritual; so would they, but with more thorough application. Thus it was that, while substantially agreeing with Hobbes as to standpoint and method, and, indeed, being indebted to him for them, they differed from him in the results they reached by these means, and claimed to have found an answer to his conclusions in the very field in which he believed himself to have established them.

1. In the first place, therefore, we remember the central point of Hobbes' doctrine of human nature. He allowed only one class of natural tendencies; they all alike aim at self-gratification, or, at least, self-preservation. Shaftesbury replies by instituting a more searching analysis. There are two classes of natural tendencies instead of only one. Some are directed to the good of others, and some are directed to the good of self. That is to say, he meets Hobbes' doctrine, that man is only and altogether selfish, by pointing out that man possesses instincts which are not selfish but social. He does not say, however, that the social affections are all good, or the selfish affections all evil. Good lies

rather in the proper adjustment of the relations between the social and the selfish affections. When a true harmony or balance between these different tendencies has been reached, the character which exhibits this balance is good. Not only so, but happiness also is produced by the same process. That individual is truly happy who will permit neither the social nor the selfish affections to obtain the mastery, but maintains them both in a state of harmonious interaction. 2. In the second place, we remember that Hobbes, in his doctrine of society, insisted that the tendency to self-gratification, even in order to attain its own ends, must be held in strict subjection to the authority of the State. The ultimate standard of morality and the supreme rule of conduct, therefore, are to be found in the command of the civil ruler. Shaftesbury, however, distinguishes between two classes of natural tendencies, the social and the selfish, and places goodness in their proper proportion. He attributes, therefore, to man a faculty of detecting this proportion. To this faculty he gives the name of "moral sense." This faculty, accordingly, affords the standard of right and wrong, provides the guidance of conduct, and becomes the impulse of action. Just as we instinctively discern the beauty of a natural scene or work of art, so we are sensible of goodness when it is presented to us in some act or character; and just as in such a matter as dress or etiquette we are guided by our native good taste, so in matters of moral conduct we are led by a certain tact, taste, or sense to pursue that path in which is to be found the balance of affections which constitutes goodness and true happiness. This moral taste also, like a taste in art, is a source of pleasure in itself, and enhances our delight in goodness, and the eagerness with which we pursue it.

A writer who followed Shaftesbury's lead is Hutcheson (1694-1747). His *Enquiry into the Original of our Ideas of Beauty and Virtue* appeared in 1720. His completed *System of Moral Philosophy* was published posthumously in 1755. He pursues the same method as Shaftesbury, and adds but little to his conclusions. He distinguishes, very much as Shaftesbury had done, between self-love and benevolence, though he identifies all virtue with benevolence in a more absolute way than Shaftesbury would have adopted. The moral sense appears as arbiter when the other affections seek to compete with benevolence. The approval of this sense adds to the pleasures of goodness. These are elaborately discussed, and Hutcheson comes to the conclusion that "the whole sum of interest lies upon the side of virtue, public spirit, and honour. To forfeit these pleasures, in whole or in part, for any other enjoyment is the most foolish bargain; and, on the contrary, to secure them with the *sacrifice* of all others is the truest gain."

§ 5. BUTLER'S ETHICAL DOCTRINE: STANDPOINT AND METHOD.

Two theories, accordingly, occupied the field of ethical study when Butler entered it: 1. That of Hobbes, according to which, (1) man was regarded as wholly selfish in every impulse and motive, (2) the absolute authority of the State was held to be the ultimate rule of conduct; 2. That of Shaftesbury, according to which, (1) benevolent as well as selfish instincts were attributed to man, (2) the ultimate rule of conduct was referred to a moral sense. Butler's own theory arises as the correction of the errors and defects of these two theories. It must be well understood, however, that, in proceeding to the task of constructing a truer doctrine, he does not abandon the standpoint occupied by the writers whom he criticises. He does not attack the presupposition upon which they proceeded; nor does he adopt a different method from that which they employed. His contention rather is that the presupposition has not been fairly dealt with, and that the method has been badly handled. The *presupposition* is that moral facts may be accurately and adequately studied as they lie within the compass of the individual mind or heart. The *method* of study is that of simple observation of the facts which will reveal themselves to any who will patiently look for them. He proposes to be true to the presupposition, and to be thorough in his use of the method. In the Preface he unfolds with great clearness the plan he means to pursue and the conception of human nature which he hopes to establish. "There are two ways," he says, "in which the subject of morals may be treated. One begins from inquiring into the abstract relations of things;[1] the other from a matter of fact, namely, what the particular nature of man is, its several parts, their economy or constitution; from whence it proceeds to determine what course of life it is which is correspondent to this whole nature. In the former method the conclusion is expressed thus, that vice is contrary to the nature and reason of things; in the latter, that it is a violation or breaking in upon our own nature. . . . The first seems the most direct formal proof, and in some respects the least liable to cavil and dispute; the latter is in a peculiar manner adapted to satisfy a fair mind, and is more easily applicable to the several particular relations and circumstances in life." " The following discourses," he goes on, "proceed chiefly in this latter method. The first three wholly. They were intended to explain what is meant by the nature of man, when it is said that virtue consists in following, and vice in deviating from it; and by explaining to show that the assertion is true." Such being the method of study, what now is the material to be studied? It is human nature. But what precisely is meant by the *nature* of a thing? What exactly is "the idea of a system, economy, or constitution of any particular nature"? " Let us instance," he says, " in a watch—suppose the several parts of it taken to pieces, and placed apart from each other: let a man have ever so exact a notion of these several parts, unless he considers the respects and relations which they have to each other, he will not have anything like the idea of a watch. Suppose these several parts brought together and anyhow united: neither will he yet, be the union ever so close, have an idea which will bear any resemblance to that of a watch. But let him view those several parts put together, or let him consider them as to be put together in the manner of a watch; let him form a notion of the relations which those several parts have to

---

[1] This method was employed by Cudworth (1617-1688). He held that there were "intelligible ideas" existing in the divine mind and communicated to the mind of man by the operation of the Spirit of God. His lofty but somewhat unpractical theory is a reflection of his life. "He spans, by his term of life, the whole period of the Stuart troubles and the Commonwealth; yet his writings might have been produced in a lonely silent monastery, instead of amid the rage of factions and the reverberation of Naseby guns." Martineau, *Types*, etc., vol. ii. p. 427.

'each other—all conducive in their respective ways to this purpose, showing the hour of the day; and then he has the idea of a watch. Thus it is with regard to the inward frame of man. Appetites, passions, affections, and the principle of reflection, considered merely as parts of our inward nature, do not at all give us an idea of the system or constitution of this nature; because the constitution is formed by somewhat not yet taken into consideration, namely, by the relations which these several parts have to each other; the chief of which is the authority of reflection and conscience. It is from considering the relations which the several appetites and passions in the inward frame have to each other, and, above all, the supremacy of reflection or conscience, that we get the idea of the system or constitution of human nature. And from the idea itself it will as fully appear, that this our nature, *i.e.* constitution, is adapted to virtue, as from the idea of a watch it appears that its nature, *i.e.* constitution or system, is adapted to measure time." Of course, as Butler observes, a watch may get out of order and keep time badly, but that is no argument against the real design of the watch. That men often, as a matter of fact, are vicious, is, therefore, no argument against the real design of their nature, which is virtue. The only difference between the man and the watch is that the watch is inanimate and passive, while the man is charged, so to speak, with keeping the machinery in good order, and is accountable for any disorder and consequent error. Butler's great aim, accordingly, is to establish this conception of human nature. When once it is clearly seen what human nature truly is, it will be seen at the same time that vice is in the strictest sense unnatural. "Thus nothing can possibly be more contrary to nature than vice; meaning by nature not only the *several parts* of our internal frame, but also the *constitution* of it. Poverty and disgrace, tortures and death, are not so contrary to it. Misery and injustice are indeed equally contrary to some different parts of our nature taken singly; but injustice is, moreover, contrary to the whole constitution of the nature." From this point of view we can understand his criticism on the two great reigning ethical theories of the day. They are alike defective in their enumeration of the elements which constitute human nature. (1) Hobbes had maintained that man had no instincts save those which led to his own private good. Against this Butler maintains the existence of other instincts leading "directly and immediately to the good of the community." The theory of Hobbes he condemns as a "partial inadequate notion of human nature." (2) Butler's study of human nature leads him to observe the presence of one principle which is superior to all others, viz. conscience, which claims absolute authority. Virtue, accordingly, is not a matter of taste or fine feeling. It is to be interpreted wholly by reference to this principle of authority. "The very constitution of our nature requires that we bring our whole conduct before this superior faculty; wait its determination; enforce upon ourselves its authority, and make it the business of our lives, as it is absolutely the whole business of a moral agent, to conform ourselves to it." Here then is the fault which Butler finds with Shaftesbury's view of human nature, "the not taking into consideration this authority, which is implied in the idea of reflex approbation or disapprobation." All that Shaftesbury has to urge in favour of virtue is that it tends best to produce happiness. But suppose, argues Butler, the case of a sceptic who should honestly disbelieve in the coincidence of virtue and happiness, how would Shaftesbury meet such a man? Plainly, he could not meet him at all. Indeed, it might be said such a man was under the obligation to be vicious; for in the absence of any other obligation, it is a man's duty to seek his own interest. Introduce, however, the principle of authority, and the case is fully met. Here suppose it should be proved that misery will follow virtue, it remains always right and necessary to do right. "Take in then that authority and obligation, which is a constituent part of this reflex approbation, and it will undeniably follow, though a man should doubt of everything else, yet, that he would still remain under the nearest and most certain obligation to the practice of virtue; an obligation implied in the very idea of virtue, in the very idea of reflex approbation."

Having thus ascertained in general the standpoint and method of Butler's doctrine, let us follow it out more in detail. We shall find that Butler's ethical teaching gathers itself up into three leading thoughts. The first is Benevolence. The second is Conscience. The third is the Love of God, which passes over from the sphere of morality into that of religion. In what follows of this introduction we shall, first of all, endeavour to summarize Butler's teaching on these points, and in so doing we shall present an abstract of the sermons bearing on these topics. Secondly, we shall exhibit certain deficiencies in Butler's views on these subjects, endeavouring to trace these to his general ethical and religious position. Finally, we shall add a few concluding remarks in which these ideas are dealt with in a more positive way.

§ 6. BUTLER'S ETHICAL DOCTRINE: STATEMENT.

A.—*Benevolence.*

Sermon I. is devoted to the discussion of this theme, and is an attempt to vindicate the disinterested character of benevolence. The thesis is that "there are as real and the same kind of indications in human nature, that we are made for society and to do good to our fellow-creatures, as that we were intended to take care of our own life, and health, and private good, and that the same objections lie against one of these assertions as against the other." His proof lies in mapping out the domain of human nature, and so exhibiting the independent position of benevolence. (1) He appeals to facts, the realities of friendship, compassion, paternal and filial affections, and all affections that terminate in the good of another. These are indisputable evidence that there is in man a principle of benevolence, as natural to him as self-love. In a long note he criticises Hobbes' reduction of benevolence to love of power, and shows conclusively that mere love of power might as easily determine the agent to cruelty as goodwill. Whether or no man possesses this principle is to be decided as any matter of natural history is decided; and by this method the result is too obvious to be missed. Man does possess this principle, although it requires cultivation and development. "This is our work: this is virtue and religion." (2) He pushes his analysis still further, and points out that there are "passions or appetites distinct from benevolence, whose primary use and intention is the security and good of society," while there are also "passions distinct from self-love, whose primary intention and design is the security and good of the individual." In an interesting note he illustrates the distinction between the general principle of self-love and the particular passions. In the rush of some special desire a man may defy the injunctions of self-love and plunge into utter ruin. Again, acting under the counsels of long-sighted self-love, directed to some distant reward, a man may crush down many of his strongest instincts. In another note he gives instances of the passions of which he speaks. Hunger is mere appetite for food, and in no sense is identical with self-love, and yet it tends to the preservation of the individual. Desire of esteem is in no sense benevolence, and yet it contributes to the good of society. In short, apart from our desire or intention, we are so constituted that in following our instinctive tendencies we become the instruments of social as well as private good. (3) He singles out that element which had been omitted in the analysis of preceding psychologists, the "principle of reflection in men by which they distinguish between, approve and disapprove, their own actions." The evidence for the existence of this principle is the same as for the existence of benevolence. The facts of life prove it. A father cares for his children from love to them, but in addition to the mere feeling he is governed by conscience. A man acts generously in one instance, meanly in another; would he, coolly reflecting on his actions without considering their consequences to himself, make no moral distinction between them? "There is therefore this principle of reflection or conscience in mankind." The conclusion of the whole matter, therefore, is that man was made for society as much as (curious that Butler never gets the length of saying "more than") for private good, and this is the root of all loyalty and patriotism. It might be asked, indeed, if man had no instincts which lead him to do evil to others. A sufficient answer to this would be the counter question, if man had no instincts which lead him to do evil *to himself.* The true solution of the puzzle is that men are sometimes so mastered by passion that they will not merely do injury to their neighbours, but will also act in manifest contradiction of their own interests. Injustice and oppression, treachery and ingratitude, are not native instincts of the soul. They are the issue of eager desire after certain good things, which even wicked people would prefer to obtain by innocent methods, if these should prove equally easy. Emulation, for instance, is "the desire and hope of equality with, or superiority over others, with whom we compare ourselves," and is a perfectly lawful sentiment. Envy, when strictly examined, is seen to have precisely the same end, only, in order to attain this end, it employs mischievous means, such as lowering the reputation of those who are our superiors, and in this consists its unlawfulness. Shame, in like manner, may prompt men to commit some crime to hide another of which they have been guilty. But obviously shame, in the first instance, tends to the welfare of the individual by keeping him back from shameful deeds. In closing this sermon, Butler illustrates with great force the truth, that so far from men always acting from dictates of self-love, they more frequently trespass on their own welfare than on that of society. Men, accordingly, have two sides to their nature, one self-regarding and another social. To neither are they perfectly true. "They are as often unjust to themselves as to others, and for the most part are equally so to both by the same actions."

B.—*Conscience.*

Sermons II., III., expound Butler's views upon conscience. His sermons are in no sense textual, but in this case he takes as starting-point the words of Paul in Rom. ii. 14, "For when the Gentiles, which have not the law, do by nature the things contained in the law, these, having not the law, are a law unto themselves." (1) In the outset he remarks that, while it is difficult, owing to the diversity which prevails among men as to right and wrong, and the inexactness of their analysis of what passes within, to determine absolutely the purpose or standard of human nature, it is, notwithstanding, possible to lay down general lines of conduct as consonant with the constitution of man. Thus, as has been pointed out in the previous sermon, there are certain principles, propensions, or instincts which lead men to do good, and these receive the sanction of conscience. Here, however, the objection might be raised that as human nature consists of various parts, a man would be acting according to his nature, and therefore according to the intention of his being, by following that particular part which happened to be at the time most imperative in its demands. Thus a man who obeyed conscience would not be morally better than the man who obeyed passion, and would have no right to blame him. The answer lies in determining more particularly what is meant by nature when we speak of following it. Two meanings are soon excluded, any principle or prompting whatever, and those which are strongest and most influence our actions. The third and true meaning is that indicated by Paul in the words which follow the text, "Which show the work of the law written in their hearts, their conscience also bearing witness, and their thoughts the meanwhile accusing or else excusing one another." To follow nature, accordingly, is not to obey any merely natural instinct, whether it be toward good or evil, but to obey the highest principle of our constitution, which alone can be a law to us. This "superior principle of reflection or conscience" has its seat in the heart of every man, and there gives forth "magisterial" sentence upon all human action. "It is by this faculty, natural to man, that he is a moral agent, that he is a law to himself." (2) To the vindication of the supremacy of this principle Butler now addresses himself. A brute creature gratifies its natural passion by snatching at the bait laid for it; and even though it destroys itself in the act, we say it acted according to its nature. A man gratifies some passion with the consequence of ruin to himself, and we say the act was unnatural, *i.e.* more precisely, there is a *disproportion* between this act and the whole nature of man. The reason of this disproportion is, that the principle of rational self-love is in itself superior to the mere temporary appetite; and so we see that among the principles which exist together in human nature, one may be naturally superior to another, and that irrespective of its mere strength. Now, apply this to conscience. A man's desire leads him to its object, even at the cost of injury to others. Conscience steps forward and, in the interest of that wider good, forbids the action. Why then is it to be obeyed? Not because of its *greater strength*, but because of its *higher authority*. The prevalence of any other principle would be a case of *usurpation*, and would do violence to the constitution. Supremacy, in fact, belongs to the very idea of conscience. Thus, in words which are most memorable, Butler proclaims his witness against an age of moral indolence and degeneracy: "Had it strength, as it has right; had it power, as it has manifest authority, it would absolutely govern the world." Think what the issue would be were we destitute of such a governor within. Then we should have to pronounce blasphemy and reverence, parricide and filial piety, equally permissible, because equally consonant with human nature, differing from each other only in respect of strength of impulse. (3) Now, at last, we have reached an adequate notion of what human nature is, and can understand what is meant when it is said that virtue consists in following it, and vice in deviating from it. Human nature resembles a civil State. It has its various departments, and these are related to one another through their common subjection to the supreme authority of conscience. If any one of these lower principles were to claim independence of conscience, and to prevail against it, this would be the violation of the constitution of man. In a note Butler admits that perfect harmony of all the parts in subjection to conscience is unattainable. All he expects is, that conscience will, on the whole, maintain its authority, and if this be done, "the character, the man, is good, worthy, virtuous." In a word, man has "the rule of right within; what is wanting is only that he honestly attend to it." Does this rule never fail? Is conscience never perplexed? To this Butler gives a very characteristic answer. He says that in a question as to whether some particular action is right or wrong, a correct decision would be given "by almost any fair man, in almost any circumstances." Conscience, therefore, thus established in man's heart is the source of moral obligation. It carries its own authority with it, is the guide given us by the Author of our being, and is to be obeyed always and at any cost. One could have wished that Butler's third sermon had closed with these deep-toned utterances. The closing paragraphs are an attempt to meet the spirit of the age with its own arguments. "Why should we impose restraints upon ourselves? Why should we be virtuous?" For answer Butler falls back on, "Because you cannot get your own good without submitting to restraint; and because, when you come to examine the matter, the highest pleasures belong to virtue, especially when it has become habitual." Conscience and self-love, duty and interest, agree in recommending the same course of life; and the man who has surrendered for conscience' sake much that the world would have called his interest, will find in the end that he "has infinitely better provided for himself, and secured his own interest and happiness."

C.— *The Love of God.*

Matthew Arnold has drawn a very suggestive parallel between Butler and the poet Gray (1716-1771). To the question why Gray, possessed as he undoubtedly was of true poetic faculty, produced so little poetry, he gives this answer: "Gray, a born poet, fell upon an age of prose. He fell upon an age whose task was such as to call forth in general men's powers of understanding, wit and cleverness, rather than their deepest powers of mind and soul. . . . Gray, with the qualities of mind and soul of a genuine poet, was isolated in his century. Maintaining and fortifying them by lofty studies, he yet could not fully educe and enjoy them; the want of a genial atmosphere, the failure of sympathy in his contemporaries, were too great." "The same thing is to be said of his great contemporary, Butler, the author of the *Analogy*. In the sphere of religion, which touches that of poetry, Butler was impelled by the endowment of his nature to strive for a profound and adequate conception of religious things which was not pursued by his contemporaries, and which, at that time and in that atmosphere of mind, was not fully attainable. . . . A sort of spiritual east wind was at that time blowing; neither Butler nor Gray could flower." In the three sermons on Human Nature, and in most of the others, we seem to feel this spiritual chill. The speaker's interest is wholly on the side of nobility and truth. He is labouring after higher views of life than those entertained by his audience. But he feels himself restrained by their want of sympathy. He forces himself to use their language, and to appeal to their dominant motives. His spirit, accordingly, rarely reaches fulness of utterance. In two sermons (XIII., XIV.), however, he does attain to some measure of freedom. His theme is the Love of God, and in dealing with it he reaches conceptions higher than the age could appreciate, higher even than the level of his own ordinary thought. Butler is here at his best ; and we begin to understand the effect he produced on those who, if they could not imitate him, expressed their admiration of his goodness by crowning him with earthly honour. Besides virtuous affections themselves, such as justice, goodness, righteousness, there is an affection for these affections " when they are reflected upon." This is the source of our love and admiration of good men. Suppose, then, a Being of perfect goodness, of vast purposes, our friend and governor, "we should, with joy, gratitude, reverence, love, trust, and dependence, appropriate the character as what we had a right in ; and make our boast in such our relation to it." But God is such a Being, as present to us, though "unseen, as our friends and neighbours." To Him, then, this affection is due. " Religion does not demand new affections, but only claims the direction of those you already have, those affections you daily feel ; though unhappily confined to objects not altogether unsuitable, but altogether unequal to them." Thus, with respect to the love of God, "we only offer and represent the highest object of an affection supposed already in your mind. Some degree of goodness must be previously supposed : this always implies the love of itself, an affection to goodness: the highest, the adequate object of this affection is perfect goodness ; which, therefore, we are to *love with all our heart, with all our soul, and with all our strength*." The love of God involves also fear, without, however, any trace of servility, and hope ; and these three, fear, hope, love, may be summed up in one word which expresses the true attitude of man the creature toward God the Creator—Resignation. Butler's language here takes leave of the eighteenth century, and recalls the glowing words of the mediæval mystic, and indeed of all who in any age have sought to realize union with God as the truth of human life. "Resignation to the will of God is the whole of piety : it includes in it all that is good, and is a source of the most settled quiet and composure of mind. . . . How many of our cares should we by this means be disburdened of ! . . . How open to every gratification would that mind be which was clear of these encumbrances !" Such a temper of mind is peculiarly suited to those who are still "in a state of imperfection." It is the highest impulse toward perfection which can be experienced by "creatures in a progress of being towards somewhat further." This "our resignation to the will of God may be said to be perfect when our will is lost and resolved up into His; when we rest in His will as our end, as being itself most just, and right, and good." And if this be so under present conditions, what shall it be when *we shall see face to face, and know as we are known?* For Butler, as for all other reverent souls, speech fails to comprehend what things God has prepared for them that love Him. He takes refuge in language which, though "first used in the early days of God's revelation," is never too old for the freshest experience of His grace: "As for me, I will behold Thy presence in righteousness: and when I awake up after Thy likeness, I shall be satisfied with it" (Ps. xvii. 16, Prayer-Book Version).

§ 7. BUTLER'S ETHICAL DOCTRINE: ESTIMATE.

The value of Butler's work is to be estimated by reference to the tone of public opinion prevalent in his day. The spirit of the age in which he lived could not be more clearly described than in his own words. It can "scarce be doubted," he says, in the opening sentences of Sermon XI. upon the Love of our Neighbour, "that vice and folly takes different turns; and some particular kinds of it are more open and avowed in some ages than in others: and, I suppose, it may be spoken of as very much the distinction of the present to profess a contracted spirit, and greater regards to self-interest than appears to have been done formerly." Against this spirit his writings are a protest, not less earnest because calmly and even coldly expressed. His aim is not that of a scientific investigator, but of a moral teacher, being, as he himself expresses it in his preface, "to obviate that scorn which one sees rising upon the faces of people who are said to know the world, when mention is made of a disinterested, generous, or public-spirited action." This ignoble temper is not confined to the eighteenth century, though it may have been its predominant characteristic; and under whatever circumstances it emerges again,

Butler's witness on behalf of a good and right that are independent of personal consequences will always remain a moral and spiritual power. If in these happier days there is a public sentiment in favour of unselfishness, if the "scorn" which troubled the preacher at the Rolls Chapel when he spoke of disinterested benevolence has given way to a sympathetic appreciation of every philanthropic effort and all forms of self-sacrifice, if instead of a cynical disbelief in any absolute good there has awakened an enthusiasm for righteousness, it is not too much to say that to these results Butler's unostentatious witness to benevolence and conscience and the love of God has contributed in no insignificant degree. While admitting and maintaining this, however, it is necessary to remark that throughout his protest against the spirit of the age he remains under the dominion of its presuppositions and its method. Between these and his own higher interests and beliefs there is a continual though unacknowledged conflict. This introduces into his teaching an element of confusion and contradiction, from which, as it was unperceived, he never wholly frees himself. He is often on the way to a higher standpoint, but the shackles of the bondage, which he himself has done much to break, are upon him, and he fails to reach the fuller and more adequate thought.

Hobbes had taught that man was, and never could be anything else than, selfish, though for obvious reasons it was his interest to subordinate in many things his private desires. This teaching found congenial soil in the generation that arose under the restored Stuart kings. It thus became an inherited conviction that man is an isolated individual self, capable of pursuing those interests alone which centre in himself, and minister to his own private advantage. A man's interest or advantage was held to be the limit of his moral horizon, beyond which he could not see, far less travel. A selfish view of man was, so to speak, in the air, just as we may say an unselfish view of man is at this present day. Disinterested benevolence was then regarded as a step *away from* man's true being, and explanations were offered to show that a man could not take this step, however much appearances might indicate that he actually did so. Disinterested benevolence now-a-days is treated as a step *toward* man's true being, and the writings of moralists are chiefly occupied with indicating how it is to be taken. The curious feature of Butler's position is that, while his whole practical interest is in the vindication of unselfishness and disinterestedness, he yet never questions the prevailing theory of man as an individual enclosed within the limits of his own private interest. His theory, which he held in common with his generation, or which at least he never offered to criticise, is continually thwarting his practical aim. His aim is to prove that man may be, and ought to be, unselfish. Immediately he is confronted by his own theory. A man must always be *himself* when he acts. If, then, he is, and cannot but be, shut up to the narrow circle of his mere individuality, his acts cannot escape the clinging taint of selfishness. When he helps his neighbour, when he acts the part of a good citizen, when he worships God, *he* remains the same rigid, self-contained individual; and all his acts, since they are *his*, remain in the last resort selfish still. In short, taking the then prevalent view of self, wherever self is present, there must also be selfishness. Self, however, must always be present, at least in all acts for which a man is responsible, even if these acts claim to be disinterested. Selfishness, therefore, must be universal, and self-love must be the supreme lord of human nature, and the source of all morality and religion. Against this conclusion Butler fights, without ever seeing that it is inevitable on the theory presupposed. All through his teaching, accordingly, self-love intervenes to disturb and perplex. Let us take each of his great ideas in turn, and endeavour to adjust them to self-love, and observe the confusion that inevitably follows.

1. Benevolence and Self-love. Butler vindicates the disinterested character of Benevolence in two ways. (1) He makes it a "blind propension." It makes for the good of our fellow-men, just as the appetite of hunger makes for food. This in Sermon I. is his answer to Hobbes, and the same view is taken in Sermons VI., VII., on Compassion. Here it is evident that Butler has saved the existence of Benevolence by robbing it of all moral quality whatever. We cannot pronounce anything good or bad which has not been the result of will to do that thing. A mere instinct is no more moral than any other mere instinct, *e.g.* the instinct to drink when we are thirsty,

even supposing its object happen to be the good of others. If giving to the poor be on a par with eating when we are hungry, obviously we have degraded Benevolence from the position of a moral quality. Many men, and perhaps more women, pride themselves on their Benevolence, while really they might as well go in to dinner with a high sense of moral rectitude for their faithfulness in doing so. Here Butler's analysis fails. He never points out the presence and operation of the will in giving moral character to our acts. (2) Butler, however, does not always regard Benevolence as a "blind propension." It is with him also a "principle of virtue." That is to say, it is a principle of action reflected upon, and consciously adopted by man. This brings him, accordingly, at once into conflict with the rival "principle" of Self-love. He wavers between two views of the relation between these two principles. In the first place, he sets them side by side on the same platform. "The proportion," he says in Sermon XII., "which the two general affections, benevolence and self-love, bear to each other . . . denominates men's character as to virtue. . . . Love of our neighbour, then, must bear some proportion to self-love, and virtue, to be sure, consists in the due proportion." To this conception of virtue as a balance or proportion he does not, however, strictly adhere. In the second place, accordingly, we find him treating Benevolence as superior to Self-love. Benevolence regarded "as a principle in reasonable creatures, and so to be directed by their reason," is "the sum of virtue." "From hence it is manifest that the common virtues and the common vices of mankind may be traced up to benevolence, or the want of it." Thus, however, he comes face to face with that conception of man as an individual which he has never questioned. Even benevolent acts are the acts of one who is *himself* in them. If that is the case, then even benevolent acts are selfish, so long as our only conception of man is that of a being, confined to the rigidly closed circle of his individual interest. Thus Butler's view of Self-love deprives his contentions on behalf of Benevolence of their real weight. Viewed "as a principle," Benevolence cannot escape the net of selfishness which the prevailing theory of man, as an individual, casts round all his actions. Its disinterestedness can be defended only by depriving it of any real moral worth, namely, by reducing it to a "blind propension."

2. *Conscience and Self-love.* Recall what is said in Sermon I. of the nature of conscience. "The mind can take a view of what passes within itself, its propensions, aversions, passions, affections, as respecting such objects, and in such degrees; and of the several actions consequent thereupon." This faculty of the mind is conscience. It is thus a faculty of judging upon the material presented to it, whether the inner motive or the consequent act. Till such material is presented to it, conscience cannot act, and has indeed nothing to do. And when the material is provided, conscience has no power to carry into effect the decisions to which, after having sifted and examined the material before it, it may have arrived. Mighty storms have raged while armies engaged in battle, without the combatants having been even aware of the fact. So also impulses contend, and passions meet in deadly strife, while overhead roll the thunders of conscience, unheeded in the empty air. "If it had only power as it has authority," is Butler's longing cry. But what is the value even of the authority of a faculty which has no power of originating action, which can present to the agent no object of pursuit? Surely the authority of such a helpless faculty is necessarily meaningless and unreal. What power is there which does present ends of action? To this there is no other answer in Butler than self-love. "Conscience and self-love, if we understand our true happiness, always lead us the same way." That is to say, man seeks and can seek only his own happiness. This is the highest end of all his actions. With reference to this, accordingly, conscience gives its decisions. This is its standard of right, its ideal good. Conscience, accordingly, in guiding men toward this goal, is acting at the behest of Self-love. And if we could conceive it possible, which it is not, that Conscience could direct men to any other end than that presented by Self-love, it would have to give way. "Religion," he remarks in Sermon XI., "is so far from disowning the principle of self-love, that it often addresses itself to that very principle, and always to the mind in that state when reason presides; and there can no access be had to the understanding, but by convincing men that the course of life

we would persuade them to is not contrary to their interest. It may be allowed, without any prejudice to the cause of virtue and religion, that our ideas of happiness and misery are of all ideas the nearest and most important to us; that they will, nay, if you please, that they ought, to prevail over those of order, and beauty, and harmony, and proportion, if there should ever be, as it is impossible there ever should be, any inconsistence between them; though those last too, as expressing the fitness of actions, are real as truth itself. Let it be allowed, though virtue or moral rectitude does indeed consist in affection to and pursuit of what is right and good as such; yet, that when we sit down in a cool hour, we can neither justify to ourselves this or any other pursuit, till we are convinced that it will be for our happiness, or at least not contrary to it." One is amazed to find so close an approximation to Hume's paradoxical formula, "Reason is and ought to be only the slave of the passions." From this the last result of his own logic Butler's strong moral sympathy restrained him; and we are left with the rough division of human nature into two parts, Self-love and Conscience, of which the former separated from the latter becomes a non-moral instinct, the latter separated from the former becomes the empty abstraction described above.

3. *Self-love and the Love of God.* Here at last, when dealing with the Love of God, we breathe an atmosphere free from all confusion and contradictions. In his sermons on this theme, Butler has escaped from the narrow limits of popular theories, to walk on mountain heights of unclouded vision. It is due, of course, in great measure to the detached sermonic form in which he has presented his results, that he rarely brings his thoughts together to weave them into systematic completeness. This is due in part to the fact of which he advertises the reader—p. 12—that no particular order was observed in selecting the sermons for publication. The want of connection, however, is due not merely to the manner in which he presents his thoughts, but to their nature. When he writes of the Love of God, he has forgotten the place which he has claimed for Self-love, Benevolence, and Conscience as independent principles of human nature, and devotes himself to the vindication of a principle

which, had he made it the standpoint whence to review the others, might have enabled him to give to each a new interpretation, and to adjust harmoniously their mutual relations. He has not sought harmony in this way. But neither has he sought it in the opposite direction, by interpreting what is noblest in man from the point of view of what is lowest in him. Herein precisely lies his interest and value as an ethical teacher. If he could not rise above the theoretic standpoint of his age, he could at least refuse its issues. The very contradictions which his teaching contains are an implicit criticism upon that standpoint, and suggest the quest for a higher; while his own higher thoughts are anticipation of success in such a pursuit.

§ 8. CONCLUDING REMARKS.

We have seen that the conception of man which prevailed in Butler's day was never theoretically criticized by him, while his practical conclusions wholly contradict it, and that, accordingly, his thought is rendered on certain points inadequate and confused. We have seen, too, that in some of his sermons he reaches a plane of spiritual and speculative thought far above that of the theories which he accepted, or at least did not explicitly controvert. The transition from the three sermons on Human Nature to those upon the Love of God is indeed the transition from the sphere of morality to that of religion. Conjecture naturally arises whether, had Butler ever reviewed the statements of the three sermons from the point of view reached in the other two on the Love of God, he would not have found it necessary to restate some of his conclusions, and so clear them from the confusions we have found to exist in them. It may prove interesting and helpful as an exercise in ethical study to deal very briefly with the three leading ideas of Butler's teaching, using by way of standpoint the suggestions contained in the higher reaches of his thought.

1. The Love of God as Ethical Motive. Individualism is not only a theory, it is an element in all human experience. The child, in the joyous life of home, has scarcely thought of himself as separate from

the loved persons with whom his life is identified. The transition from childhood to manhood is marked by an intense consciousness of separation, in which the individual, often assertively and disagreeably, vindicates his independence and claims his rights. The unconscious unity of the child-life is broken. The man knows himself as a distinct individual, standing in the might of his self-assertion over against nature, humanity, God. When he realizes his position at its point of deepest significance, namely, in relation to God, he finds it to be not merely pain, but sin. He *ought to be* at one with this God from whom he is keenly aware he is separate. He knows in his inmost soul that his separation from God, and all consequent acts of trespass against God, are his own doing, the burden of whose guilt lies upon his own head alone. He knows, too, that his utmost efforts to regain union with God are necessarily ineffective, for the reason which becomes obvious on reflection, namely, that he is himself separate from God, and that to all his actions there clings the taint of this state of separation, which is a state of sin. Action conducted within the sphere of mere morality is, at best, merely an approximation, never an attainment. Morality, *per se*, is endless process, and that means ceaseless dissatisfaction. The very sense of failure, however, contains the germ of hope; for, obviously, only a being meant for union with God could feel pain in separation from Him. Union with God is at once the expectation and the latent presupposition of morality. It is also the fundamental fact of religion, the proclamation of which constitutes "glad tidings" to all who labour under the weight of an unrealized and unrealizable ideal of goodness. The life of Christ is not merely a display of sinlessness, it is the positive achievement of righteousness in the very sphere wherein man has already hopelessly failed. The death of Christ has accomplished the reconciliation with God which is the goal of the human spirit, and starting from which alone man can advance to a victorious solution of the moral problem. There exists, therefore, as actual fact a life which is the union of God and man, after which man has yearned. Here the contradictions and dissatisfactions of man's moral effort are seen to be absent; in their place, a perfect harmony of the human will and the divine. If, however, that life lay wholly beyond the sinner, a spectacle to be gazed at by him with longing eyes, while he felt himself debarred for ever from its appropriation, it would merely add to his misery. The question therefore remains, How can he make it his own? Butler's answer is, "By resignation." More fully and adequately the answer may be given, "By surrender." What keeps you from Christ, and union with God in Him? Nothing but Self, to which you live, and in whose limits you are shut up as in a living death. Die, then, to that Self which is death, and so for the first time begin to live. Yield yourself a living sacrifice to God. Accept that will of God which was fulfilled for you on the Cross, and this you cannot truly do without yourself also dying on that Cross. Thus, to die with Christ is at the same time to rise with Him into newness of life. Whereas once to you to live was Self, now that Self is dead, and to you to live is Christ. That Self is dead. It is no longer yours nor you. It was sin-laden and under condemnation; now you have escaped the imputation of its guilt. It was toiling at an impossible task, seeking through individual effort to reach a goodness that for ever fled before it; now you have arrived at that "blessed goal." Christ speaks in gracious assurance, " You are delivered from failure. Goodness is your heritage in me. Go forth, no more in weariness, but gladly, triumphantly, restfully, to achieve in the world that which is already yours." Reconciliation is the "basis of ethics." The Love of God, fulfilled in redemption, and waking in man a glad response, is the only adequate ethical motive.

2. *Conscience as Power and Authority.* Butler in his teaching on Conscience is the prophet of the eighteenth century, proclaiming to a cynical and selfish generation the supremacy of the rule of right within. In two respects, however, as we have seen, the claim which he makes for Conscience is invalidated. First, it is confessed that conscience has no *power*. It is a mere faculty of judgment. It depends upon other faculties to present the material upon which it is to judge. It cannot of itself, apart from the material thus presented to it, fix any end of pursuit for man. Second, this involves further that the faculty, which has no *power*, can have no real *authority*. It acts, and sometimes Butler admits, can act, only in the interest of self-love, and selects only the ends which self-love proposes. Its supposed supremacy, therefore, becomes practical

servitude. All this is inevitable from the point of view of that psychology which was Butler's unquestioned presupposition, the logical issues of which are presented in Hume. If all elements of knowledge, and all ends of actions, are presented in sensations, which it is the work of thought merely to compare and combine, we shall soon be brought to see that knowledge is no more than the aggregate of associated sensations, and virtue is obedience to the strongest passions. And when we see this we shall be brought to question the presupposition which has led us to this conclusion, and we shall ask once more the "tyro's question," How is experience possible? and we shall seek new conditions both of knowledge and morality. If Butler did not put this question to himself, he at least, as we have seen, made a fore-grasp at the answer. From the religious standpoint which he reaches in some of his sermons we gather that the good is not the calculated result of a process of comparison and abstraction carried on by the faculty of conscience. It is the will of God, whose end may be variously expressed as His own glory or the good of men. We are good when we are identified with this Supreme Will, when our wills are lost and resolved into it. This includes "all that is of good." Will not such a conception significantly modify that view of Conscience which Butler has elsewhere taught, and to which it is noteworthy he does not recur in his sermons on the Love of God?

1. Conscience will be quite other than a faculty of judgment, exercised on a material given to us from without. The purpose of God, as it moves towards its divine event, realizes itself in various spheres of ethical conduct, *e.g.* the family, the State, etc., and is therein so far revealed. Man, however, is more than the theatre whereon this purpose is to be displayed. His perfection is indeed the end aimed at, and this can be achieved only as he recognises the good, and devotes himself to it freely as its instrument. The good, therefore, is revealed not only *in* and *by* man, but also *to* him. It is in fact his deepest consciousness, that with which, when he knows himself, he will know himself to be one. It is impossible, therefore, to speak of conscience as a bit of man, a "part" of human nature, one "faculty" among others. It is the man himself, as he responds

to the good which is present to him even when he fails to recognise it, and which constitutes his true nature. Or, what is the same thing from the other side, it is the Spirit itself bearing witness with our spirits that we are citizens and heirs of the kingdom which is righteousness, and therefore peace and joy.

2. Hence, also, the authority of conscience must be differently conceived. Its authority does not belong to itself as a mere faculty, but to the good of which it is the apprehension. In hearkening to conscience, therefore, we are not listening to the deliverances of any faculty of ours, but to the voice of God, who, as He has revealed Himself in the manifold fulness of the world, which is the sphere of moral attainment, thus also bears witness to Himself in our consciousness. In obeying conscience we are not acknowledging the mere issue of a calculation, we are identifying ourselves with that will which has created the ends which it proposes for our pursuit, and which as we yield ourselves to it becomes in us the energy of their attainment. We need not, therefore, with Butler regret the disparity between the authority of conscience and its power. As a mere faculty it has neither one nor other. As the presence to our spirits of the Supreme Will, which has created the moral universe, and through us seeks the fulfilment of its infinite design, it is the highest authority, the most absolute power. In acting according to conscience, we are rising above the region of moral paralysis in which we for ever balance feeling against feeling, vainly seeking the good in the product, and are entering through surrender into union with the good which claims us for itself, whose organs and instruments we become, and whose victory is our certain heritage. Conscience, accordingly, may in this respect be compared to faith, as its character has been defined in Reformation theology. Faith is no independent faculty with authority or power of its own. It has in itself no saving efficacy. In believing, we receive Christ, and are made one with Him; then He saves and sanctifies. Even so, conscience is no independent faculty, and has, as Butler truly says, no power whatever to produce moral conduct. In acting according to conscience, we receive the will of God, and become one with it; then He commands, and is Himself the energy of obedience. It is interesting to notice the parallel between Butler's

view of conscience and his view of faith, as this incidentally appears in a conversation with Wesley. The subject of discussion is the doctrine of justification, and Butler remarks, "Why, sir, our faith itself is a good work; it is a virtuous temper of mind." The individual, therefore, is the architect of his own fortunes, even in matters spiritual, and Butler shrinks from any view of the touch of the Divine Spirit upon the human as tending to delusion. In this conversation he further remarked that "the pretending to extraordinary revelations and gifts of the Holy Spirit was a horrid thing—a very horrid thing." Conscience and faith alike, therefore, are independent faculties, by the excercise of which the individual achieves moral and spiritual wellbeing for himself. From this it follows that the failure of Conscience to select what is right among many possible ends of action, and the failure of Faith to choose Christ as the object of worship and service, are cases of mere failure for which the man cannot be held responsible, any more than for short-sightedness or any other instance of an imperfect faculty. Where, however, we deprive Conscience and Faith of their fancied dignity as faculties, and regard them simply as expressions of man's spiritual energy, laying hold in the one case on the will of God, in the other on the Person of His Son, we begin to realize the tremendous imperative of duty, the infinite claim of Christ. In action we have to do, not with the inference of a faculty, but the presence of an Almighty Will revealing itself to the soul. "To him," therefore, "that knoweth to do good and doeth it not, to him it is sin;" not mistake or failure merely, but trespass against the Supreme Will in devotion to which our moral wellbeing consists. In belief, in like manner, we are not concerned with any intellectual propositions or logical demonstrations, but with the claim of a Person who is present to our spirits as truth and light. Faith in Christ, therefore, is not intellectual accuracy, therefore also rejection of Christ is not intellectual error; it is the failure to yield to One who is claiming us for Himself, is endowing us with His own perfect manhood. To violate Conscience and to reject Christ are acts destructive of our moral and spiritual wellbeing. They cannot truly be estimated in terms of our limited understanding. The blame and the loss are alike infinite.

3. **Benevolence as Virtue.** The question which the popular sentiment of the day put to Butler was, How can a man seek any good save his own? We have seen that Butler, in endeavouring to vindicate the reality of Benevolence as a principle of human nature, is hampered by his narrow and individualistic conception of self. As long as this conception is retained, and a man's self is regarded as a circle rounded upon itself and exclusive of all other individualities, it will be a ceaseless puzzle how a man can get out of himself to identify himself with anything beyond himself. The answer comes only on lines to which Butler introduces us when, forgetting his psychological presuppositions, he rises to the thought of God, and so for the first time begins to apprehend human nature. With the first dawn of the consciousness of self there wakes the demand for self-satisfaction. But the self which thus claims the world for its own, while at the same time it refuses to go forth of itself, is not our true self. As we yield to it and do it homage and seek to satisfy its ceaseless craving, it is our false self, the evil genius of our life, continually dragging us into sin, and denial of our true nature. We come to ourselves only when this false self is slain. By death we are born again. Our true self rises in Him with whom through surrender we are one. The man Christ Jesus is the truth of human nature. Our own good is now to be interpreted by reference to Him who is our true self. The good for us is the attainment of that supreme purpose with which we are now identified, and in whose service we find perfect freedom. But that purpose has for its goal salvation, that is to say, the elevation of men to the highest excellence of which their nature, physical, social, spiritual, is capable. It is, in a word, "goodwill to men." It is therefore to the extent in which he makes this his aim, and seeks to achieve the good of his fellow-man, that a man finds his own. So far, therefore, from its being impossible for a man to seek any good save his own, he can only find his own in the pursuit of that of others. That *is* his good ; for *he* is much more than a centre of private interest. His true nature finds its issues along all the lines of the love of God. By every deed in which self is crucified to rise again in service that seeks no reward, in suffering that knows no murmur, he becomes more truly himself, and reaches

toward that ideal of humanity which is real in Christ, and will be realized in all who are one with Him.

In closing, we learn from Butler that the supreme principle of human nature is the will of God, and by this we interpret each special aspect of it, and adjust their relations with one another. This, as we receive it in deep surrender, wakes in us as a passion which becomes the impulse and the energy of all ethical attainment. This, as it bears witness to itself in us through conscience, commands us with that absolute authority which belongs only to a law that is the expression of infinite love. This, as we yield ourselves its servants, reaches a result in which the good of our fellow-men and that of ourselves are achieved together in indissoluble unity of thought and fact. It is true, indeed, that at any point of present attainment there open upon us visions of profounder surrender, more perfect obedience, more Christ-like charity. When such revelations break upon our soul there cannot be but pain, but there must not be despair. Our pain is the throb within us of that living will which is bearing us toward its own divine event, and which cannot fail us till it has purged away from us every discordant element, and made of us with itself one infinite harmony. Thus, amid the anguish of crucifixion we enjoy His peace who gives not as the world giveth, and amid the darkness of a vision that sees not yet *sub specie eternitatis*, can rest in confidence on His word.

> "O living will that shalt endure,
>   When all that seems shall suffer shock
>   Rise in the spiritual rock,
> Flow through our deeds and make them pure.
>   That we may lift from out of dust
>   A cry as unto Him that hears,
>   A cry above the conquered years,
>   To one that with us works and trust,
>   With faith that comes of self-control,
>   The truths that never can be proved,
>   Until we close with all we loved,
>   And all we flow from, soul in soul."

THREE SERMONS.

SERMON I.

UPON HUMAN NATURE.

"For as we have many members in one body, and all members have not the same office; so we, being many, are one body in Christ, and every one members one of another."—ROM. xii. 4, 5.

THE Epistles in the New Testament have all of them a particular reference to the condition and usages of the Christian world at the time they were written. Therefore, as they cannot be thoroughly understood unless that condition and those usages are known and attended to, so, further, though they be known, yet, if they be discontinued or changed, exhortations, precepts, and illustrations of things, which refer to such circumstances now ceased or altered, cannot at this time be urged in that manner and with that force which they were to the primitive Christians. Thus the text now before us, in its first intent and design, relates to the decent management of those extraordinary gifts[1] which were then in the Church (1 Cor.

---

[1] *Decent management of those extraordinary gifts.* Chapters xii., xiii., xiv. of the First Epistle to the Corinthians deal with the subject of the *charismata* or special gifts of the early Christian Church. Abuses soon crept in. The Glossolalia, or gift of tongues, was specially liable to abuse. In their frenzy the worshippers fell into strange intellectual and spiritual confusion, and might even be heard blaspheming the blessed name of the Saviour (1 Cor. xii. 3). Paul seeks to check these hideous extravagances by pointing out that however varied the gifts might be in their distribution and exercise, their service and aim were one. All alike are gifts of the same Spirit, who, through them all, carries on His holy operations (vers. 4–11). This Paul then illustrates

xii.), but which are now totally ceased. And even as to the allusion that "we are one body in Christ," though what the apostle here intends is equally true of Christians in all circumstances, and the consideration of it is plainly still an additional motive, over and above moral considerations, to the discharge of the several duties and offices of a Christian; yet it is manifest this allusion must have appeared with much greater force to those who, by the many difficulties they went through for the sake of their religion, were led to keep always in view the relation they stood in to their Saviour who had undergone the same; to those who, from the idolatries of all around them and their ill-treatment, were taught to consider themselves as not of the world in which they lived, but as a distinct society of themselves, with laws, and ends, and principles of life and action quite contrary to those which the world professed themselves at that time influenced by. Hence the relation of a Christian was by them considered as nearer than that of affinity and blood, and they almost literally esteemed themselves as members one of another.[2] It cannot, indeed, possibly

---

by the analogy of the body and the members. The members are many, and have various functions; but they are members of one body, and work together in perfect harmony and mutual dependence (vers. 12-27). Butler's aim in this sermon is to vindicate the independence and importance of benevolence. He finds, accordingly, a convenient starting-point in this conception of a variety, which does not lead to rivalry or disunion, being controlled by a higher principle of unity.

[2] They almost literally esteemed themselves as members one of another. The words of Jesus (Matt. xxiii. 8), "One is your Master, even Christ; and all ye are brethren," are not a metaphor or hyperbole. They express the literal fact. Sin, separating as it does man and God, does thereby also separate man from man. Redemption, uniting as it does man and God, does thereby also unite man and man. The brotherhood of man can be fully understood only through the conception of redemption, and is practically recognised only by that religion which rests upon the fact of the accomplished redemption of the world. Christ, accordingly, announces His task as the foundation of the kingdom of God, which tolerates no external distinctions of race or rank, and comprehends humanity in the privilege and obligation of brotherhood. "Here," *i.e.* in the kingdom, "the Gentile met the Jew, whom he had been accustomed to regard as the enemy of the human race; the Roman met the lying Greek sophist; the Syrian slave the gladiator born beside the Danube. In brotherhood they met, the natural birth

be denied that our being God's creatures, and virtue being the natural law we are born under, and the whole constitution of man being plainly adapted to it, are prior obligations to piety and virtue [3] than the consideration that God sent His Son into the world to save it, and the motives which arise from the peculiar relations of Christians as members one of another under Christ our head. However, though all this be allowed, as it expressly is by the inspired writers, yet it is manifest that Christians, at the time of the Revelation, and immediately after, could not but insist mostly upon considerations of this latter kind.

These observations show the original particular reference of the text, and the peculiar force with which the thing intended by the allusion in it must have been felt by the primitive Chris-

---

and kindred of each forgotten, the baptism alone remembered in which they had been born again to God and to each other." *Ecce Homo*, p. 128, 14th ed.

[3] **Prior obligations to piety and virtue.** Butler's defence of benevolence is pervaded by a thoroughly Christian interest. He is, however, so penetrated by the spirit of his age that he seeks, apart from religion, for grounds and motives of those very virtues which religion chiefly inculcates. We have also always to remember in reading Butler, when we are tempted to complain of his cold and "moderate" language, that he is dealing with those over whom Christianity as a faith had ceased to exert any influence. His conscious purpose, therefore, is to establish virtue on a basis of its own apart from the support of religion. Yet he himself leads us to see that morality is complete in religion alone, and that from the standpoint of religion alone it can be satisfactorily vindicated. It may seem, indeed, an intellectual subtlety to say that religion is the basis of morality, when so many people who make no religious profession live thoroughly moral lives. It is plain, however, that there is a distinction between *acting morally* and *being moral*. We may *act morally*, under the constraint of law, whether it be the law of public opinion or the law of God, and yet between our wills and the law there may be no real union. But we can *be moral* only when our wills are in thorough harmony with the law, that is to say, when they are one with the supreme will which utters itself in the law. We now act as the organs of that higher will which works in us "to will and to do." Our moral action is now the issue of our religious life. To be truly moral is possible only when we are truly religious, *i.e.* when our wills are surrendered to and mastered by the supreme will. To those who love morality, Christ is offered as the one condition on which they can have their noblest ambitions satisfied.

tian world. They likewise afford a reason for treating it at this time in a more general way.

The relation which the several parts or members of the natural body have to each other and to the whole body, is here compared to the relation which each particular person in society has to other particular persons and to the whole society; and the latter is intended to be illustrated by the former. And if there be a likeness between these two relations, the consequence is obvious: That the latter shows us we were intended to do good to others, as the former shows us that the several members of the natural body were intended to be instruments of good to each other and to the whole body. But as there is scarce any ground for a comparison between society and the mere material body,[4] this without the mind being a dead, inactive thing; much less can the comparison be carried to any length. And since

---

[4] **Comparison between society and the mere material body.** Herbert Spencer would not agree with Butler's statement that the comparison could not be "carried to any length." He himself goes great lengths in such a comparison, basing his procedure on the thesis that "the permanent relations among the parts of a society are analogous to the permanent relations among the parts of a living body." Apart from Spencer's use of the comparison, it is one which certainly will often be found useful in illustrating the characteristics of a society. The living body presents the picture of a unity prevailing amid many diverse parts; and this is precisely the kind of unity which exists in society, the individuals composing it being "members one of another." In the case of the living body, however, the unity is imperfect, since the parts still remain physically separate from one another. In society the unity is of a higher order, for here each part, *i.e.* each individual, lives *in* the whole of which he is a member, and is what he is by his place in it; while only in so far as he lives *for* it, and makes the welfare of the whole and of each member his own individual purpose, does he attain the fulness of his own being. Even in various types of society we notice an advance toward the perfect harmonization of whole and part. The family is such a type. The State is another. The kingdom of God is the highest and only perfect type. The child lives in and for the family, but does so unconsciously. The citizen of the State lives in and for the community; but inasmuch as no earthly community, however well regulated, is perfect, he lives also a life apart from it. Only in the kingdom of God does man find for every power of body, soul, and spirit full and satisfactory exercise, and for his whole being an entire consecration which leaves no room for self, while at the same time his personality is not thereby endangered, but developed in richest contents and noblest proportions.

the apostle speaks of the several members as having distinct offices, which implies the mind, it cannot be thought an allowable liberty, instead of the *body* and *its members*, to substitute the *whole nature of man, and all the variety of internal principles which belong to it*. And then the comparison will be [5] between the nature of man as respecting self, and tending to private good, his own preservation and happiness; and the nature of man as having respect to society, and tending to promote public good, the happiness of that society. These ends do indeed perfectly coincide; and to aim at public and private good are so far from being inconsistent, that they mutually promote each other; yet, in the following discourse, they must be considered as entirely distinct; otherwise the nature of man, as tending to one or as tending to the other, cannot be compared. There can no comparison be made without considering the things compared as distinct and different.

From this review and comparison of the nature of man as respecting self and as respecting society, it will plainly appear that *there are as real and the same kind of indications in human nature that we were made for society and to do good to our fellow-creatures, as that we were intended to take care of our own life, and health, and private good; and that the same objections lie against one of these assertions as against the other.* For—

---

[5] **And then the comparison will be.** Butler is afraid to press the analogy of the body and its members too far. He accordingly fixes his attention on "the whole nature of man." In this are to be observed two aspects, "the nature of man as respecting self," and "the nature of man as having respect to society." Between these he proposes to institute a comparison, the issue of which he here states as the doctrine to be developed through detailed examination. It is true that in the end Butler hopes to show that man's private interest is bound up in, and indeed is identical with, the public good. In the meantime, however, he regards these two aspects of human nature as distinct. Jevons has the following remarks on *comparison* and *analogy*. Comparison is "the action of mind by which we judge whether two objects of thought are the same or different in certain points." Analogy, strictly defined, "is not an identity of one thing with another, but an identity of relations. In the case of numbers, 7 is not identical with 10, nor 14 with 20, but the ratio of 7 to 10 is identical with the ratio of 14 to 20, so that there is an analogy between these numbers. In ordinary language, however, analogy has come to mean any resemblance between things which enables us to believe of one what we know of the other."

First, There is a natural principle of *benevolence* (*a*)⁶ in man,

---

(*a*) Suppose a man of learning to be writing a grave book upon human nature, and to show in several parts of it that he had an insight into the subject he was considering; amongst other things, the following one would require to be accounted for: the appearance of benevolence or goodwill in men towards each other in the instances of natural relation and in others.¹ Cautious of being deceived with outward show, he retires within himself to see exactly what that is in

---

⁶ **A natural principle of benevolence.** We have in Butler no proper doctrine of the will, and without this much of his contending on behalf of virtue must fall to the ground. A principle which is merely *natural*, just as it is natural to eat when we are hungry, can scarcely be characterized as good or bad. Only when our natural tendencies are taken up and employed by our wills are the actions which result capable of being estimated in terms of good or bad, or ourselves as agents capable of being either approved or condemned. The distinction appears, quaintly and forcibly expressed in Sir Thomas Browne's *Religio Medici*. Speaking of this very principle of benevolence, the amiable physician declares that he is "delineated and naturally framed to such a piece of virtue." "This general and indifferent temper of mine," he proceeds, "doth more nearly dispose me to this noble virtue; ... yet if we are directed only by our particular natures, ... we are but moralists; divinity will still call us heathens. Therefore this great work of charity must have other motives, ends, and impulsions. I give no alms only to satisfy the hunger of my brother, but to fulfil and accomplish the will and command of my God; I draw not my purse for his sake who demands it, but for His that enjoyed it. I relieve no man upon the rhetorik of his miseries, nor to content mine own commiserating disposition; for this is still but moral charity, and an act that oweth more to passion than to reason. He that relieves another upon the bare suggestion and bowels of pity, doth not this so much for his sake as for his own, and so, by relieving them, we relieve ourselves also." Of course it is not meant that we are not good when we do good, if we happen to take pleasure in it. Feeling as such has nothing to do with goodness. There is nothing good save a will which recognises the good that is revealed to it, and yields itself up to that in heartiest surrender. The claim of Christianity is that the service of Christ includes the highest possible good for man. It accordingly addresses itself specially to those who love goodness, and bids them yield their wills to Christ, that their lives may be the systematic achievement of goodness, not the spasmodic pursuit of mere instincts and "natural principles" of virtue.

---

¹ [Hobbes, *On Human Nature*, c. ix. § 7.]

which is in some degree to *society* what *self-love* is to the *indi-*

---

the mind of man from whence this appearance proceeds, and, upon deep reflection, asserts the principle in the mind to be only the love of power,[7] and delight in the exercise of it. Would not everybody think here was a mistake of one word for another? That the philosopher was contemplating and accounting for some other human actions, some other behaviour of man to man? And could any one be thoroughly satisfied that what is commonly called benevolence or goodwill was really the affection meant, but only by being made to understand that this learned person had a general hypothesis to which the appearance of goodwill could no otherwise be reconciled? That what has this appearance is often nothing but ambition; that delight in superiority often (suppose always) mixes itself with benevolence, only makes it more specious to call it ambition than hunger of the two; but in reality that passion does no more account for the whole appearance of goodwill than this appetite does. Is there not often the appearance of one man's wishing that good to another which he knows himself unable to procure him; and rejoicing in it, though bestowed by a third person? And can love of power any way possibly come in to account for this desire or delight? Is there not often the appearance of men's distinguishing between two or more persons, preferring one before another to do good to, in cases where love of power cannot in the least account for the distinction and preference? For this principle can no otherwise distinguish between objects than as it is a greater instance and exertion of power to do good to one rather than to another. Again, suppose goodwill in the mind of man to be nothing but delight in the exercise of power: men might indeed be restrained by distant and accidental considerations; but these restraints being removed, they would have a disposition to and delight in mischief as an exercise and proof of power. And this disposition and delight would arise from, or be the same principle in the mind as, a disposition to and delight in charity. Thus cruelty, as distinct from envy and resentment, would be exactly the same in the mind of man as goodwill: that one tends to the happiness, the other to the misery of our fellow-creatures, is, it seems, merely an accidental circumstance, which the mind has not the least regard to. These are the absurdities which even men of capacity run into when they have occasion to belie

---

[7] **The love of power.** This is the form which self-interest usually takes in Hobbes. He applies it in different directions to explain the various phases of moral experience. Pity is "the *imagination* or *fiction* of future calamity to ourselves, proceeding from the sense of *another* man's calamity." Laughter is "nothing else but *sudden glory* from some sudden *conception* of some *eminency* in ourselves, by comparison with the *infirmity* of others, or with our own formerly." Consistently with this, religion is defined as "fear of power invisible."

vidual. And if there lie in mankind any disposition to friendship:[8] their nature, and will perversely disclaim that image of God which was originally stamped upon it; the traces of which, however faint, are plainly discernible upon the mind of man.

If any person can in earnest doubt whether there be such a thing as goodwill in one man towards another (for the question is not concerning either the degree or extensiveness of it, but concerning the affection itself), let it be observed that *whether man be thus or otherwise constituted, what is the inward frame in this particular* is a mere question of fact or natural history, not provable immediately by reason. It is therefore to be judged of and determined in the same way as other facts or matters of natural history are: By appealing to the external senses or inward perceptions respectively as the matter under consideration is cognizable by one or the other: by arguing from acknowledged facts and actions; for a great number of actions of the same kind in different circumstances, and respecting different objects, will prove to a certainty what principles they do not, and, to the greatest probability, what principles they do proceed from. And, lastly, by the testimony of mankind. Now, that there is some degree of benevolence amongst men may be as strongly and plainly proved in all these ways as it could possibly be proved, supposing there was this affection in our nature. And should any one think fit to assert that resentment in the mind of man was absolutely nothing but reasonable concern for our own safety, the falsity of this, and what is the real nature of that passion, could be shown in no other ways than those in which it may be shown that there is such a thing, in *some degree*, as *real* goodwill in man towards man. It is sufficient that the seeds of it be implanted in our nature by God. There is, it is owned, much left for us to do upon our own heart and temper; to cultivate, to improve, to call it forth, to exercise it in a steady, uniform manner. This is our work, this is virtue and religion.

---

[8] **Friendship.** The reality of such a position is proved, not only by the existence of such classic examples as David and Jonathan, or Damon and Pythias, but by the universal experience of the race. Sacred are the ties of blood, by which those born into the circle of one family are held together; yet they often prove powerless against the accident of separation, or the strain of diverse temperaments, and brothers drift into utter strangeness. In a very obvious sense it is true that "there is a friend that sticketh closer than a brother." Friendship, being the deliberate choice of two independent personalities, by which each renders the other love and trust and service, will sometimes be found more enduring and more rich in spiritual meaning than any mere natural relationship. Holy and beautiful are the bonds of love in which two become "one flesh;" yet such love, by the very fact that it exists between two who are one, has lost the

if there be any such thing as compassion,[9] for compassion is

---

quality of disinterestedness. Friendship, standing on a lower plane, existing between those who are still separate in their way of life, and yet maintaining a loving trust, and rejoicing in service and surrender, holds a position of unique dignity and excellence. It is a test of the quality of love, being indeed, as has been said, "love, without either flowers or veil." He who is incapable of genuine friendship cannot be true either in brotherhood or in the marriage relationship; while the truer a man is to his friends, the better will he fulfil the obligations of all other ties. Friendship in its highest exercise of surrender forms the type of a love that is more than human. "Greater love hath no man than this, that a man lay down his life for his friends." When such love has been exhibited in act, there could be no higher honour than to be introduced into its fellowship. "Henceforth," says One in whom this love dwelt in its fulness, "I call you not servants; . . . but I have called you friends."

[9] **Compassion.** Literally, according to its derivation, "a suffering with another." Butler in his fifth sermon thus analyses our state of mind in presence of human misery. "There are often three distinct perceptions or inward feelings upon the sight of persons in distress: real sorrow or concern for the misery of our fellow-creatures; some degree of satisfaction from a consciousness of our freedom from that misery; and as the mind passes on from one thing to another, it is not unnatural from such an occasion to reflect upon our own liableness to the same or other calamities." It is this last feeling which Hobbes has singled out and made the whole of compassion. Commenting on the words, "Rejoice with them that do rejoice, and weep with them that weep," Butler remarks that "though men do not universally rejoice with all whom they see rejoice, yet, accidental circumstances removed, they naturally compassionate all, in some degree, whom they see in distress, so far as they have any real perception or sense of that distress: insomuch that words expressing this latter, pity, compassion, frequently occur; whereas we have scarcely any single one by which the former is distinctly expressed." The function of compassion he describes in Sermon VI. as that of an "advocate within us," "to gain the unhappy admittance and access, to make their case attended to." "Pain and sorrow and misery have a right to our assistance: compassion puts us in mind of the debt, and that we owe it to ourselves as well as to the distressed." There are three words whose close relations and precise distinctions it is interesting to note, though difficult to state accurately: compassion, οἰκτιρμός; mercy, ἔλεος; grace, χάρις. They form an ascending scale of dignity and moral beauty. Compassion is, as Butler here says, "momentary love;" or, in Martineau's words, "the feeling that springs forth at the spectacle of suffering," arising instantly "at the mere inspection of misery." The object of compassion is misery as such, irrespective

momentary love; if there be any such thing as the paternal or filial affections;[10] if there be any affection in human nature, the

---

of how it has been produced; and is felt by us merely as human beings identifying ourselves with a fellow-creature's woe. Mercy, in like manner, has regard to misery, disaster, or loss; but it is distinguished from compassion in that the misery is regarded as the consequence of the sufferer's act. A bystander may *compassionate* the plight of an accused person; but it belongs to the judge or the prosecutor to have *mercy* on him. Mercy is the prerogative of one to whom Law or Right or Might has conferred power over another. "Blessed are the merciful: for they shall obtain mercy." Happy those who, in the power of love, rose above bare law or force, and so dealt with their fellow-men, as they shall wish they had dealt when they themselves stand helpless at the bar of infinite justice. Verily they shall not be disappointed. Grace is distinguished from compassion and mercy by the position of him who displays it in relation to those upon whom it is conferred. Grace implies that the person displaying it is not compelled to his acts of benevolence by any outward necessity. He is absolutely free to give or to withhold as seems good to him. Such freedom is chiefly to be found in persons of exalted rank. We speak thus most naturally of the grace of a king. To speak of grace in the conduct of one who is our social equal, we feel to be an exaggeration, tolerable only in moments of impassioned feeling. The word, accordingly, belongs by first right to God. He alone is free in the true sense; for He acts by the inner necessity of His love. His grace is bestowed upon those who have no right or title to it. Exalted above them in His holiness, He yet freely bestows His grace upon them in their sin. God's *grace* looks upon men as sinners, "who forgiveth all our iniquities." His *mercy* deals with them as miserable by consequence of their sin, "who healeth all our diseases." His *compassion* is the throb of infinite love at sight of the need of man; hence this word occurs with exquisite monotony in the narrative of the ministry of Jesus.

[10] **Paternal or filial affections.** The Family does, indeed, supply magnificent proof of the essentially social nature of man. In his recent work on *Social Aspects of Christianity*, Canon Westcott has given accurate and beautiful expression to this thought: "Man, in a word, is made by and made for fellowship. The Family and not the individual is the unit of mankind. This fact is the foundation of human life, to which we must look for the broad lines of its harmonious structure. And we shall not look in vain. For the Family exhibits, in the simplest and most unquestionable types, the laws of dependence and trust, of authority and obedience, of obligation and helpfulness, by which every form of true activity is regulated. The Family enables us to feel that the destination of all our labours, the crown of all our joys, the lightening of all our sorrows, the use of all our

object and end of which is the good of another: this is itself benevolence, or the love of another. Be it ever so short, be it ever so low a degree, or ever so unhappily confined, it proves the assertion, and points out what we were designed for as really as though it were in a higher degree and more extensive. I must, however, remind you that though benevolence and self-love [11] are different, though the former tends most directly to

---

endowments, is social. . . . In the Family, as has been nobly said, *living for others* becomes the strict corollary of the patent fact that we *live by others.*" The special idea of Fatherhood, he proceeds, is "the correlative responsibilities of government and devotion hallowed by love." "Fatherhood is, I have said, the pattern, or, to repeat the phrase I have used before, the original sacrament of authority; sonship, of reverence and obedience. The necessity of the relation lies in the harmony of our constitution. If it were not so, and we must face the alternative, order could only be maintained by selfish fear, or by no less selfish hope."

[11] Benevolence and self-love. Sermon XI. deals with this subject of the coincidence of benevolence and self-love. Butler there maintains that benevolence is a "particular passion," and stands in this respect on the same footing with ambition, revenge, and all other "particular passions." "Thus it appears that there is no peculiar contrariety between self-love and benevolence; no greater competition between these than between any other particular affections and self-love." The only question can be, "whether there be any peculiar contrariety between the respective courses of life which these affections lead to; whether there be any greater competition between the pursuit of private and of public good, than between any particular pursuits and that of private good." Butler then proceeds to examples: "Thus one man's affection is to honour as his end; in order to obtain which he thinks no pains too great. Suppose another, with such a singularity of mind, as to have the same affection to public good as his end, which he endeavours with the same labour to obtain. In case of success, surely the man of benevolence hath as great enjoyment as the man of ambition; they both equally having the end their affections, in the same degree, tended to: but in case of disappointment, the benevolent man has clearly the advantage; since endeavouring to do good, considered as a virtuous pursuit, is gratified by its own consciousness, *i.e.* is in a degree its own reward." Viewed, further, "as forming a general temper," he asks, "is benevolence less the temper of tranquillity and freedom than ambition or covetousness? Does the benevolent man appear less easy with himself, from his love to his neighbour? Does he less relish his being? Is there any peculiar gloom seated on his face? Is his mind less open to entertainment, to any particular gratification? Nothing is more manifest

public good and the latter to private, yet they are so perfectly coincident, that the greatest satisfactions to ourselves depend upon our having benevolence in a due degree; and that self-love is one chief security of our right behaviour towards society. It may be added that their mutual coinciding,[12] so that we can scarce

than that being in good humour, which is benevolence whilst it lasts, is itself the temper of satisfaction and enjoyment." Looking, therefore, to these and other sources of gratification peculiar to the benevolent, "self-love," he adds, "methinks should be alarmed. May she not possibly pass over greater pleasures than those she is so wholly taken up with?" The comparison of self-love and benevolence as to the amount of enjoyment procurable from each, leaves benevolence at least not behind self-love. The only real competition between the two, or interference of the one with the other, relates "much more to the materials or means of enjoyment, than to enjoyment itself." And even here benevolence has not much to fear. "Thus as to riches: so much money as a man gives away, so much less will remain in his possession. Here is a real interfering. But though a man cannot possibly give without lessening his fortune, yet there are multitudes might give without lessening their own enjoyment; because they may have more than they can turn to any real use or advantage to themselves." We have already had occasion to remark that this proof of the coincidence of self-love and benevolence, while useful as a mere reply to selfishness, is not the strength of Butler's position, and rather weakens than helps his vindication of conscience.

[12] **Their mutual coinciding.** Mere coincidence does indeed bring us no further than this, that we are made both for social and for private ends. Butler, however, himself helps us to go farther. Our highest good and the satisfaction of our true nature is attained when we have died to our mere separate self, and when we have yielded ourselves to the will of God, which is the good of man. Not only, therefore, do self-love and benevolence coincide, but self-love satisfies itself only in benevolence. Not only are we made for social as well as private good, but we reach private good only by living for social good. The effort to live for private good alone is in fact suicidal; not the attainment, but the destruction of our own welfare. "He that findeth his life shall lose it; and he that loseth his life for my sake shall find it." All experience is an education in this great idea. We are members of the Family; and there, by a sweetly unconscious training, we learn the lesson of that surrender which is our truest weal. We are members of Society; and in the duties of friendship and neighbourhood we learn more consciously to identify ourselves with our fellowmen, and in their good to seek our own. By an extension of the same discipline we learn that our lives are bound up with those of all who with us are children of humanity, and that our good is but part of a universal heritage. This good is no shadowy abstraction. It is a

promote one without the other, is equally a proof that we were made for both.

Secondly, This will further appear from observing that the several *passions* and *affections* which are distinct (*a*) both from

---

(*a*) Everybody makes a distinction between self-love and the several particular passions,[13] appetites, and affections; and yet they are often confounded again. That they are totally different will be seen by any one who will distinguish between the passions and appetites *themselves,* and *endeavouring* after the means of their gratification. Consider the appetite of hunger, and the desire of esteem; these being the occasion both of pleasure and pain, the coolest *self-love,* as well as the appetites and passions themselves, may put us upon making use of the *proper methods of obtaining* that pleasure and avoiding that pain; but the *feelings themselves,* the pain of hunger and shame, and the delight from esteem, are no more self-love than they are anything in the world. Though a man hated himself, he would as much feel the pain of hunger as he would that of the gout; and it is plainly supposable there may be creatures with self-love in

---

purpose committed to the hands of a Redeemer, and by Him fulfilled. The discipline of life, therefore, leads to the love of Christ as the interpretation of all its enigmas, and the inspiration of all noble endeavour.

" Life with all it yields of joy and woe,
And hope and fear,
Is just our chance o' the prize of learning love,
How love might be, hath been indeed, and is."

[13] Self-love and the several particular passions. The distinction thus stated is much insisted on by Butler. In this note he first points out the distinction between the particular passions, simply as feelings, and self-love. A man who hated himself would be distressed if he suffered the pain of hunger. There have been found those in whom self-love was so developed that they were indifferent to the praise or blame of their fellows. The "particular passions" of hunger and the desire of esteem are thus seen to be wholly distinct from self-love. He then remarks on the difference in the actions which result from particular passions and from self-love respectively. The man who yields himself up to the particular passion of strong drink, and who is led thereby to destroy his home, wreck his prospects, and undermine his health, is manifestly not acting from self-love. He is obviously his own worst enemy. A man who, in hope of some great reward, of the special nature of which he is ignorant, devotes himself to laborious toil, is manifestly not acting under the impulse of some particular passion. He is obviously impelled by the general principle of self-love.

benevolence and self-love, do, in general, contribute and lead us

them to the highest degree, who may be quite insensible and indifferent (as men in some cases are) to the contempt and esteem of those upon whom their happiness does not in some further respects depend. And that self-love and the several particular passions and appetites are in themselves totally different, so that some actions proceed from one and some from the other, will be manifest to any who will observe the two following very supposable cases: One man rushes upon certain ruin for the gratification of a present desire; nobody will call the principle of this action self-love. Suppose another man to go through some laborious work upon the promise of a great reward, without any distinct knowledge what the reward would be; this course of action cannot be ascribed to any particular passion. The former of these actions is plainly to be imputed to some particular passion or affection, the latter as plainly to the general affection or principle of self-love. That there are some particular pursuits or actions concerning which we cannot determine how far they are owing to one and how far to the other, proceeds from this, that the two principles are frequently mixed together, and run into each other. The distinction is further explained in the eleventh sermon.[14]

---

[14] **Explained in the eleventh sermon.** The relative passage is as follows: "Every man hath a general desire of his own happiness, and likewise a variety of particular affections, passions, and appetites, to particular external objects. The former proceeds from or is self-love, and seems inseparable from all sensible creatures who can reflect upon themselves and their own interest or happiness, so as to have that interest an object to their minds: what is to be said of the latter is, that they proceed from, or together make up, that particular nature according to which man is made. What the former pursues is somewhat internal, our own happiness, enjoyment, satisfaction; whether we have, or have not, a distinct, particular perception of what it is, or wherein it consists: the objects of the latter are this or that particular external thing which the affections tend towards, and of which it hath always a particular idea or perception. The principle we call self-love never seeks anything external for the sake of the thing, but only as a means of happiness or good: particular affections rest in the external things themselves. One belongs to man as a reasonable creature reflecting upon his own interest or happiness. The others, though quite distinct from reason, are as much a part of human nature." The use which Butler makes of this distinction in the eleventh sermon is to defend the disinterested nature of benevolence. As a particular affection it tends toward and rests in its object, viz. the good of others. It does so as a mere instinct. Self-love has no more connection with benevolence than with any other instinct. It will naturally suggest the propriety of

to public good as really as to *private*. It might be thought too minute and particular, and would carry us too great a length, to distinguish between, and compare together, the several passions or appetites, distinct from benevolence, whose primary use and intention is the security and good of society; and the passions distinct from self-love, whose primary intention and design is the security and good of the individual.(*a*). It is enough to the

---

(*a*) If any desire to see this distinction and comparison [15] made in a particular instance, the appetite and passion now mentioned may serve for one. Hunger is to be considered as a private appetite; because the end for which it was given us is the preservation of the individual. Desire of esteem is a public passion; because the end for which it was given us is to regulate our behaviour towards society. The respect which this has to private good is as remote as the respect that it has to public good; and the appetite is no more self-love than the passion is benevolence. The object and end of the former is merely food; the object and end of the latter is merely esteem; but the latter can no more be gratified without contributing to the good of society, than the former can be gratified without contributing to the preservation of the individual.

---

gratifying this instinct as well, *e.g.*, as that for food. In the above note Butler is seeking to show in general that there are certain instincts in our nature which carry us, without our intention, to the good of others; so that, by the very framework of our constitution, it is evident that we are meant for public as well as private good. It is in passages like the above that we feel most keenly the want in Butler of a doctrine of the will, or any proper conception of self-determination. Benevolence as a mere instinct has no higher moral worth than hunger. Benevolence is a virtue only when, being fully conscious of ourselves, we freely yield ourselves to the service of others. Mere instinct has no place in action which can be pronounced good or bad, for which we can be praised or blamed. When we act we must be ourselves, either the self clung to in its isolation, which is a false, bad self, or the self *surrendered* to a good beyond itself, and therefore *found* therein in truth and fulness. We can scarcely blame Butler, however, for the deficiencies of a psychology in which he had been bred, and out of which he has had his own share in leading us.

[15] **This distinction and comparison.** Among the various instincts and particular passions which make up no inconsiderable part of human nature, there are some which tend to private good, and yet cannot be identified with self-love; and there are others which tend to public good, and yet cannot be identified with benevolence. The appetite of hunger is quite distinct from self-love; and yet it tends toward the preservation of individual life. The desire of esteem is quite distinct from benevolence; and yet it tends to developing the common weal. The conclusion

present argument that desire of esteem from others, contempt and esteem of them, love of society as distinct from affection to the good of it, indignation against successful vice, that these are public affections or passions, have an immediate respect to others, naturally lead us to regulate our behaviour in such a manner as will be of service to our fellow-creatures. If any or all of these may be considered likewise as private affections, as tending to private good, this does not hinder them from being public affections too, or destroy the good influence of them upon society, and their tendency to public good. It may be added, that as persons without any conviction from reason of the desirableness of life would yet, of course, preserve it merely from the appetite of hunger; so, by acting merely from regard (suppose) to reputation, without any consideration of the good of others, men often contribute to public good. In both these instances they are plainly instruments in the hands of another —in the hands of Providence—to carry on ends, the preservation of the individual and good of society, which they themselves have not in their view or intention. The sum is, men have various appetites, passions, and particular affections, quite distinct, both from self-love and from benevolence; all of these have a tendency to promote both public and private good, and may be considered as respecting others and ourselves equally and in common; but some of them seem most immediately to respect others, or tend to public good; others of them most

---

which Butler draws from this psychological study is that, simply as we are constituted, and apart from any conscious purpose of ours, we are meant to serve, and actually do serve, a public as well as a private end. It is necessary to note a confusion which occurs in Butler's representations of benevolence. In the eleventh sermon, as the passage quoted above shows, he ranks benevolence among the instincts and particular affections which are all alike to be distinguished from self-love. In this section of the first sermon he classes self-love and benevolence together as conscious regulative principles of action, and contrasts with them certain instincts which, while distinct from them, tend to the advantage of the individual or the good of society. Which is benevolence, then, an instinct or a principle? And if the latter, how is it related to its rival self-love? From these difficulties the individualistic conception of man, which Butler never questioned, permits no escape. Butler only casts them aside when, forgetting his individualism, he rises to the conception of a supreme will, surrender to which is our first duty, and the necessary condition of our self-realization.

immediately to respect self, or tend to private good. As the
former are not benevolence, so the latter are not self-love;
neither sort are instances of our love either to ourselves or
others, but only instances of our Maker's care and love both of
the individual and the species, and proofs that He intended we
should be instruments of good to each other, as well as that we
should be so to ourselves.

Thirdly, There is a principle of reflection [16] in men, by which

---

[16] **A principle of reflection.** The term "reflection" is part of the philosophical terminology of John Locke (1632–1704), whose *Essay concerning Human Understanding* was published in 1690. According to Locke, all the ideas which we have in our minds are derived from one or other of two sources: *sensation*, which is the perception of outward objects by means of the senses; or *reflection*, which is the perception of what is present in the soul. Reflection has nothing to do with the objects presented to it beyond noting and classifying them. It has no originative power whatever. This, which as Locke used it was chiefly a theory of knowledge, is taken over by Butler without question, and applied to morals. Just as, according to Locke, the mind simply observes the objects of knowledge presented to it; so, according to Butler, the mind "takes a view" of the material of motive and desire, the propensions, aversions, etc., which offer themselves before it. In this case, as in the other, the mind is wholly unoriginative. It can neither create ends of action nor modify them when they are presented to it. It can only approve one, disapprove another, and with respect to a third remain in the paralysis of indifference. Hence Butler is forced to lament that with all its authority conscience is powerless.

Obviously our theory of knowledge and our theory of morals must go hand in hand. Any imperfection we may discover in the one will suggest a corresponding deficiency in the other. Any modification we may make in the one will suggest a corresponding correction in the other. If we are dissatisfied with Locke's theory of knowledge, we are forced to see the deficiency of Butler's doctrine of conscience. If we are led, say by Butler himself, to a higher view of our moral constitution, we must seek in consistency another conception of knowledge. If, in knowledge, the mind clothes the objects presented to it in its own forms, and so creates the intellectual world in which we live, then, in action, it will have the same creative energy, will frame the objects of our endeavour into its own image, and will lead us to their triumphant realization. The world of things knowable and the world of moral action are alike the revelation of mind, spirit, God. We enter the kingdom of truth and the kingdom of righteousness alike *sub personâ infantis*. Yielding the false independence of thought and will, we reach the vision of the true, we become organs

they distinguish between, approve, and disapprove their own actions. We are plainly constituted such sort of creatures as to reflect upon our own nature. The mind can take a view of what passes within itself, its propensions, aversions, passions, affections,[17] as respecting such objects, and in such degrees, and of the several actions consequent thereupon. In this survey it approves of one, disapproves of another, and towards a third is affected in neither of these ways, but is quite indifferent.[18] This

---

and instruments of the good. When this surrender is complete, we know as we are known, we are perfect as our Father in heaven is perfect.

[17] **Propensions, aversions, passions, affections.** The first two of these terms imply an instinctive tendency of nature acting from within, and finding in outward objects no more than a mere occasion. Thus the desire of food is a propension, the need arising apart from the object, though, when the object is presented, there is an immediate forth-going of our nature toward it. An aversion is in like manner an instinctive shrinking of our nature from some external object. In the case of passions and affections, however, the outward object is more than the mere occasion of the feeling, and is rather the cause. Passions and affections are indeed literally the modes in which we suffer something from outward objects, or are affected by them. In the case of passions, the objects repel us; in the case of affections, they attract. Fear is a passion. Love is an affection.

[18] **Is quite indifferent.** Is this possible? Are there any actions of which we cannot say that they are right or wrong? Butler's view of conscience as a faculty of calculation leads him to say that there are. Conscience sitting in judgment, with what goes on in the mind before it, declares of some of these propensions, aversions, etc., and the actions that proceed from them, that they conduce to the good of the individual or of society. Of others it declares that they have a tendency to the opposite effect. Of a third class it can say nothing, because they appear to have no bearing whatever upon the good of the individual or of society. If, however, conscience has a position at once more glorious and more humble, if it be no independent faculty, but the revelation in consciousness of the Highest Good, the supreme Will of God, which omits nothing from its sway, but penetrates through every department of the moral sphere, we see that toward no action can conscience be indifferent, because there is none in which the Highest Good may not be done or the Will of God not be honoured. Hence follows the duty of conscientious self-examination. Every action, however incidental or habitual, ought to be scrutinized to see whether and how far in it the Will of God is being done. It is possible, of course, to make our very conscientiousness a sin, and to be so very careful that *we* should be good, that the good itself remains

undone. Instead of this morbid feeling, we admire the wholesome disregard of self shown in those who seek noble ends, and forget to count over their faults and failings as they follow on.

> " Time was, I shrank from what was right,
> From fear of what was wrong ;
> I would not brave the sacred fight,
> Because the foe was strong.
>
> But now I cast that finer sense
> And sorer shame aside.
> Such dread of sin was indolence,
> Such aim at heaven was pride.
>
> So when my Saviour calls, I rise,
> And calmly do my best ;
> Leaving to Him, with silent eyes
> Of hope and fear, the rest.
>
> I step, I mount where He has led ;
> Men count my haltings o'er ;—
> I know them ; yet, though self I dread,
> I love His precept more."
>
> JOHN HENRY NEWMAN.

Apart from any such marked misuse, the discipline of self-scrutiny is of inestimable value in the development of character. It leads us to do things which no one would have blamed us for leaving undone. Those things which constitute our ordinary tasks we do "not with eye-service, as men-pleasers, but in singleness of heart, as unto the Lord," and therefore we reach an excellence of workmanship impossible otherwise. We create new obligations for ourselves as we see new means of extending the good whose nature we now more perfectly apprehend. Above all, the disparity, which our growth in goodness only makes more apparent to us, between our imperfect attainment and God's mighty purpose, is the impulse of a profounder surrender to Him, a more complete dedication to His service. When this process of examination has been completed with respect to any particular action, the judgment at which we arrive can only be one or other of two things. It has been right ; or, it has been wrong ; in either case, infinitely. It has been right ; then we know it not to have been our individual deed, and therefore we can claim no merit for it. It was the deed of that righteous purpose to which we have yielded ourselves, and which works through us as instruments. "Without me ye can do nothing," is the Divine Voice to us. "Not unto us, O Lord, not unto us," is the answer of our spirits. Or, it has been wrong ; then we know it to be our act, our very own, done by us in defiance of the Good which claimed us. From the point of view of the moral judgment, there is no distinction of greater or less in

temper, and actions, is conscience;[19] for this is the strict sense of the word, though sometimes it is used so as to take in more. And that this faculty tends to restrain men from doing mischief to each other, and leads them to do good,[20] is too manifest to need

---

respect to wrong. There is but one standard, and that is the highest; and every act, however trifling, is an occasion in which we may or may not comply with this standard. It was our testing time, when we might have shown our loyalty to Good and God. If we failed, there lies upon us the whole guilt of antagonism to the Good, of rebellion against God. Any transgression is in its own nature infinite. Repentance, therefore, must be in like manner measureless. Therefore also any wrong present in the moral world is an absolute barrier in the way of the final achievement of good. Wrong as such can neither be overlooked nor amended. It demands to be dealt with by way of atonement. Then follows forgiveness and amendment.

[19] **Conscience.** Conscience is fundamentally knowledge. The object of this knowledge is the Good, or the Will of God. The occasion upon which this knowledge awakes is some action which we perform. The sentence in which we express our knowledge is that our action has or has not conformed to the Good which ought to have been achieved in it. This knowledge may be obscured by passion or self-will. At length the Good which has been seeking to penetrate the mists which wrapped us round, breaks upon us like the sun through a bank of clouds; and we see things clearly—the ideal of good as it shines upon us, our act in its failure to reach the ideal, ourselves in our personal responsibility. Thus Peter blundered on, from cowardly evasion to downright lying and rudest blasphemy, till that Look fell upon his soul which filled it with an awful light of judgment. Then he saw the Good he had disowned, his deed in its foul ingratitude, himself laden with unspeakable transgression. If, then, Conscience is to perform for us its destined function, we must not treat it as a lonely oracle which of itself will always give a true response. It needs to be ceaselessly developed and educated through constant study of the Good or Will of God in all its manifestations. Such manifestations are to be found in the history of the race, and specially in the history of grace whose record is in the Scriptures, in the constitution and government of the society of which we are members, in the providences, engagements, and tasks of our daily life, in the immediate voice of God through His Spirit to our souls. By reverent study of the Will of God thus revealed, Conscience becomes purged from error, and permits us to look over the field of life with calm and certain gaze.

[20] **Leads them to do good.** Conscience, when brought to bear on acts of natural impulse, has a twofold result. In the first place, it binds the isolated and spasmodic acts into the unity of a fixed habit, so that there is now a continuous operation on behalf of what is good. In

being insisted upon. Thus a parent has the affection of love to his children: this leads him to take care of, to educate, to make due provision for them. The natural affection leads to this; but the reflection that it is his proper business, what belongs to him, that it is right and commendable so to do: this added to the affection, becomes a much more settled principle, and carries him on through more labour and difficulties for the sake of his children than he would undergo for that affection alone, if he thought it, and the course of action it led to, either indifferent or criminal. This, indeed, is impossible,—to do that which is good, and not to approve of it; for which reason they are frequently not considered as distinct, though they really are: for men often approve of the actions of others, which they will not imitate, and likewise do that which they approve not. It cannot possibly be denied that there is this principle of reflection or conscience in human nature. Suppose a man to relieve an innocent person in great distress; suppose the same man afterwards, in the fury of anger, to do the greatest mischief to a person who had given no just cause of offence; to aggravate the injury, add the circumstances of former friendship and obligation from the injured person: let the man who is sup-

---

the second place, the habit thus formed, when it is conscientiously maintained, elevates the ideal of good and strengthens the impulse toward it, and thus inspires the performance of yet higher and nobler actions. Thus, to take Butler's example, a father feels for his children a natural impulse of affection. As mere impulse, it acts spasmodically, irrationally. Suppose conscience to awake. Then, first, his occasional acts are welded into a habit, and in this way are freed from the errors of their spasmodic appearance, and are made to tell directly and continuously on the welfare of his family. And, second, this formation of a habit of attending to his children's interests does not destroy the impulse of his affection; rather does it, under the guidance of Conscience, give to his fatherly love deeper intensity and nobler aim, and so render him capable of deeds of self-sacrifice which his first undisciplined instinct had been too weak to achieve. According to one ancient saying, "Virtue is Knowledge;" according to another, "Virtue is Habit." Both are true. Virtue is Knowledge; knowledge of the Good, and surrender to it. Virtue is Habit; in so far as the principle of good enters into the raw material of instinct and desire, and forms it into an organized body of orderly and habitual good conduct; and this habit in turn forms a platform for a nearer and fuller vision of the ideal, a starting-point for its yet more earnest pursuit.

posed to have done these two different actions coolly reflect upon them afterwards, without regard to their consequences to himself;—to assert that any common man [21] would be affected in the same way towards these different actions, that he would make no distinction between them, but approve or disapprove them equally, is too glaring a falsity to need being confuted. There is therefore this principle of reflection or conscience in mankind. It is needless to compare the respect it has to private good with the respect it has to public; since it plainly tends as much to the latter as to the former, and is commonly thought to tend chiefly to the latter. This faculty is now mentioned merely as another part of the inward frame of man, pointing out to us in some degree what we are intended for, and as what will naturally and of course have some influence. The particular place assigned to it by nature, what authority it has, and how great influence it ought to have, shall be hereafter considered. From this comparison of benevolence and self-love, of our public and private affections, of the courses of life they lead to, and of the principle of reflection or conscience as respecting each of them, it is as manifest that *we were made for society and to promote the happiness of it, as that we were intended to take care of our own life and health, for private good.* And from this whole review must be given a different draught of human nature [22]

---

[21] **Any common man.** Any common man in this age and country would condemn the conduct Butler describes. Yet we cannot infer from this that in every man, savage and civilised, pagan and Christian, there exists a faculty capable of declaring at once with respect to any action whether it be right or wrong. In the history of the race there has been a growing revelation of righteousness; and conscience as the witness in man to this righteousness has grown with the growing revelation. In estimating the morality of a past stage of this development we are neither to condemn it, because it fails to reach our standard, nor so to twist its record that it shall seem to reach our standard. Conscience, therefore, will approve at one stage what it will condemn at another. Yet these differences between the conscientious convictions of one age or people and those of another do not discredit the existence or the reliability of conscience. There is conscience in man, the witness in man to that good which he is meant to reach; and this witness has become fuller and clearer as the good has been increasingly revealed through the medium of growing experience.

[22] **A different draught of human nature.** The three great facts of Benevolence, and those instincts which apart from Benevolence

from what we are often presented with. Mankind are by nature
so closely united, there is such a correspondence between the
inward sensations of one man and those of another, that disgrace is as much avoided as bodily pain, and to be the object of
esteem and love as much desired as any external goods : and,
in many particular cases, persons are carried on to do good to
others, as the end their affections tend to and rest in ; and
manifest that they find real satisfaction and enjoyment in this
course of behaviour. There is such a natural principle of
attraction in man towards man, that having trod the same
track of land, having breathed in the same climate, barely having
been born in the same artificial district or division, becomes the
occasion of contracting acquaintances and familiarities many
years after ; for anything may serve the purpose. Thus
relations, merely nominal, are sought and invented, not by
governors, but by the lowest of the people ; which are found
sufficient to hold mankind together in little fraternities and
copartnerships : weak ties indeed, and what may afford fund
enough for ridicule, if they are absurdly considered as the real
principles of that union ; but they are, in truth, merely the
occasions, as anything may be of anything, upon which our
nature carries us on according to its own previous bent and bias ;
which occasions, therefore, would be nothing at all were there not
this prior disposition and bias of nature. Men are so much one
body [23] that in a peculiar manner they feel for each other shame,

---

make for the good of others, and Conscience, have thus led Butler to
a conception of human nature directly the reverse of that which had
been expounded by Hobbes, and which formed the ordinary basis of
popular philosophizing. Hobbes' "draught of human nature" was a
sufficiently terrible one. Cf. his description of the state of nature,
quoted in the Introduction, p. 22.

[25] **So much one body.** Hobbes had regarded men as a heap of
warring atoms requiring to be reduced into order by the strong
compulsion of authority. Butler regards men as united after the
similitude of a body, all the parts being mutually interdependent,
sharing a common experience, living for and by a common weal. It
must have been strong meat for his hearers at the Rolls Chapel, this
powerful statement, not of the criminality, though that is, of course,
implied, but of the absurdity of selfishness. It is indeed not the
highest tone that might be assumed. Nevertheless in dealing with
those who glory in their shame and are impervious to higher impulse,
it is legitimate to urge that selfishness, judged even by its own
standard, does not and cannot pay. A man may, if he will, refuse the

sudden danger, resentment, honour, prosperity, distress; one or another, or all of these, from the social nature in general, from benevolence, upon the occasion of natural relation, acquaintance, protection, dependence; each of these being distinct cements of society. And, therefore, to have no restraint from, nor regard to others in our behaviour, is the speculative absurdity of considering ourselves as single and independent, as having nothing in our nature which has respect to our fellow-creatures, reduced to action and practice. And this is the same absurdity as to suppose a hand, or any part, to have no natural respect to any other, or to the whole body.

But allowing all this, it may be asked, "Has not man dispositions and principles within which lead him to do evil to others as well as to do good? Whence come the many miseries else which men are the authors and instruments of to each other?" These questions, as far as they relate to the foregoing discourse, may be answered by asking, "Has not man also dispositions and principles within which lead him to do evil to himself as well as good? Whence come the many miseries else, sickness, pain, and death, which men are the instruments and authors of to themselves?"

It may be thought more easy to answer one of these questions than the other, but the answer to both [24] is really the same: that

---

exercise of benevolence, the obligations of kinship or acquaintance. It may be impossible to convict him of wrong; but he ought at least to understand that his conduct has not the excuse of self-interest, and that his course of action is fatal to that very individual benefit for the sake of which he declines to help his fellow. Selfishness is, in fact, as Butler points out, not less a blunder than a crime, which long ago St. Paul expressed in a parable which supplies Butler in this passage with his leading metaphor. "As the body is one, and hath many members, and all the members of that one body, being many, are one body: so also is Christ. . . . The eye cannot say unto the hand, I have no need of thee: nor again the head to the feet, I have no need of you. . . . And whether one member suffer, all the members suffer with it; or one member be honoured, all the members rejoice with it" (1 Cor. xii. 12, 27).

[24] **The answer to both.** Butler now meets a supposed objection: "Men, as a matter of fact, do evil to one another; how then are they meant for social good?" To this Butler retorts: "Men, as a matter of fact, do evil to themselves; will it therefore be urged that they are not meant for self-love?" The true solution of the difficulty lies in this, that men have passions which they insist on gratifying, without

mankind have ungoverned passions which they will gratify at any rate, as well to the injury of others as in contradiction to known private interest; but that as there is no such thing as self-hatred, so neither is there any such thing as ill-will in one man towards another, emulation and resentment being away, whereas there is plainly benevolence or good-will; there is no such thing as love of injustice, oppression, treachery, ingratitude, but only eager

---

considering how such conduct will affect others or even themselves. Butler is thus led to the position that there is in man no natural tendency to do evil to others. This position he then supports by instancing and briefly examining certain instincts or tendencies which might seem to imply an innate impulse in man to do evil to his fellow. 1. Ill-will. According to a recent writer, we have an original instinct of antipathy, which is not in itself morally evil. Let this be fostered and indulged, however, and it becomes a fixed determination of the will, accompanied by a settled flow of feeling, and issuing in habitual lines of action. The mere instinctive antipathy is now Ill-will or Malice. Its ordinary expression is Censoriousness. One of its commonest products is Slander. "The original antipathy, whose indulgence matures into this type of malice, may have only the most trivial excuse; yet be none the less bitter for beginning with dislike of some petty personal peculiarity of physiognomy, or speech, or manner,—a curve in the nose, a colour of the hair, a sniffle in the voice, a smile too much, or an address too curt. The subject of such aversions becomes the slave of his own prejudices. He enjoys the idea of the objectionable person in ridiculous positions, or caught in contemptible actions; and is ready to seize this enjoyment on the faintest hint of an hypothesis, so as to pass without scruple from supposition to belief, and from belief to assertion. This is probably the natural history of the great majority of slanders. They are born of the malice of prejudice more often than from the deliberate purpose of supplanting a rival or avenging a defeat" (Martineau, *Types of Ethical Theory*, vol. ii. p. 173). 2. Injustice. The legal definition of justice is, " constans et perpetua voluntas suum cuique tribuendi;" and law will define this *suum* in detail for each case submitted to its decision. The man, however, who rises above the mere prescription of law will recognise that his neighbour has a claim upon him apart from the terms of some special legal contract, a general claim to have *his* welfare considered when his fellows are laying plans to secure their own. Hence there arises, as the late Prof. Green has pointed out, a "refinement" in the sense of justice, which leads the lover of justice to inquire " as to any action that may suggest itself to him, whether the benefit he might gain by it for himself, or for some one in whom he is interested, would be gained at the expense of any one else, however indifferent to him personally, however separated from him in family,

desires after such and such external goods, which, according to a very ancient observation, the most abandoned would choose to obtain by innocent means if they were as easy and as effectual to

status, or nation" (*Prolegomena*, p. 224). The essence of injustice, accordingly, is disregard of our neighbour's claim to be considered. The love of injustice would be a positive zest for depriving our neighbour of his rights, and for so acting that he would suffer loss. Oppression, treachery, ingratitude, are all forms of injustice, in so far as they all involve disregard of that good which, though it be that of another, ought to be the object of our sacred care. Our neighbour's freedom is to be defended as our own; his purposes are to be guarded by our loyalty; his love is to have the response of our own. That men naturally delight in violating one another's sanctity in these respects is what Butler denies. His view is that men do eagerly desire to attain certain objects for themselves, and that this desire, cherished till it become an irresistible passion, will sweep them into deeds of wrong foreign to their natural disposition. The question whether men naturally delight to do evil is theological rather than ethical. There can be no doubt, however, that the natural history of many famous crimes has been such as Butler here sketches. First, there is the eager desire for some object of ambition. Second, there is the perception or suggestion of some deed of cruelty or wrong as necessary to secure the wished-for prize, and in many instances this has been accompanied by a shock of surprise and indignation as the better spirit of the man recoiled from the idea. Then there ensues a more or less prolonged period of struggle in which the intense desire for the object gradually extinguishes all lingering compunctions, till finally the deed is done from which at first there had been so much shrinking. The classical example in literature is Macbeth as portrayed by the master-hand of Shakespeare. He wishes the crown. He sees the deed which is necessary to procure it for him, the murder of King Duncan; but would rather, in some impossible way, his own hands should be clean. His wife, prior to the deed at any rate, has far fewer "compunctious visitings" than he, and sketches his character for him with pitiless analysis :—

> "Thou wouldst be great;
> Art not without ambition, but without
> The illness should attend it: what thou wouldst highly.
> That wouldst thou holily; wouldst not play false,
> And yet wouldst wrongly win: thou'dst have, great Glamis,
> That which cries, '*Thus thou must do, if thou have it;*'
> *And that which rather thou dost fear to do,*
> *Than wishest should be undone.*"

3. Emulation and envy. Butler has in view the definition given by Hobbes, which is as follows : " Griefe for the successe of a competitor, if joyned with endeavours to enforce our own abilities to equal or excel

their end; that even emulation and resentment by any one who will consider what these passions really are in nature (*a*), will be found nothing to the purpose of this objection, and that the

---

(*a*) Emulation is merely the desire and hope of equality with, or superiority over others, with whom we compare ourselves. There does not appear to be any *other grief* in the natural passion, but only *that want* which is implied in desire. However, this may be so strong as to be the occasion of great *grief.* To desire the attainment of this equality or superiority by the *particular means* of others being brought down to our own level, or below it, is, I think, the distinct notion of envy. From whence it is easy to see that the real end which the natural passion, emulation, and which the unlawful one, envy, aims at, is exactly the same, namely, that equality or superiority; and consequently, that to do mischief is not the end of envy, but merely the means it makes use of to attain its end. As to resentment, see the eighth sermon.

---

him, is emulation; if joyned with endeavours to supplant or hinder, envie." In opposition to this, Butler denies that there is any grief occasioned by the success of a competitor. All that man naturally feels under such circumstances is the desire to equal or excel him. If, however, we seek to attain to this equality or superiority, not by our own legitimate effort, but by reducing others to our own level or below it, this is envy. Here in this case, however, our aim is not to do mischief to others. The mischief we do them is simply the means we use to equal or excel them. That man is moved by emulation or even by envy does not prove, therefore, according to Butler, that he has any innate grief at his neighbour's good, or any innate desire to diminish it. 4. Resentment. The following passages from Sermon VIII. contain an outline of Butler's views on this topic:— "Resentment is of two kinds: hasty or sudden, or settled and deliberate.... Sudden anger, upon certain occasions, is mere instinct; as merely so as the disposition to close our eyes upon the apprehension of somewhat falling into them, and no more necessarily implies any degree of reason.... It is opposition, sudden hurt, violence which naturally excites the passion; and the real demerit or fault of him who offers that violence, or is the cause of that opposition or hurt, does not, in many cases, so much as come into thought.... But from *this deliberate anger, or resentment*, is essentially distinguished, as the latter is not naturally excited by or intended to prevent mere harm without appearance of wrong or injustice." Resentment proper, therefore, is felt with respect to injurious persons, and as such "is one of the common bonds by which society is held together; a fellow-feeling which each individual has in behalf of the whole species as well as of himself.... The natural object or principles and passions in the mind of men, which are distinct both from self-love and benevolence, primarily and most directly lead to right behaviour with regard to others as well as himself, and only secondarily and accidentally to what is evil. Thus though men, to avoid the shame of one villany, are sometimes

---

occasion of settled resentment then being injury, as distinct from pain or loss, it is easy to see, that to prevent and to remedy such injury, and the miseries arising from it, is the end for which this passion was implanted in man. It is to be considered as a weapon, put into our hands by nature, against injury, injustice, and cruelty." Of course it is liable to abuses, which Butler further particularizes. Still, its existence in human nature is no proof that we naturally do hurt to one another; rather is it one of those primary instincts which tend to regulate social life in justice and equity. "Anger," it has been said, "is one of the sinews of the soul; he that wants it hath a maimed mind, and with Jacob, sinew-shrunk in the hollow of his thigh, must needs halt. Nor is it good to converse with such as cannot be angry."

Anger becomes criminal where it is divorced from its real function, and is directed, not against violations of justice and goodness, but against injuries levelled as we suppose at our individual self. Resentment thus indulged seeks not the vindication of outraged right, but vengeance upon the insolent being who has wounded our pride. In this sense it is identical with murder, according to the teaching of the New Testament: "He that hateth his brother is a murderer." For such sin the most profound ethical teachers have marked out the most fearful punishment as no more than well deserved. It startles us to hear from the lips of Christ that "whosoever shall say, Thou fool, shall be in danger of hell-fire," till we reflect that the sin implied is a murderous assault upon the brother's spiritual manhood. Quite in the same vein of ethical estimate of sin, Dante, we find, beneath the abodes of the licentious, the gluttonous, the prodigal, and the avaricious, in the foul waters of the Stygian lake, places the wrathful and the gloomy, the former condemned to brutish strife, the latter to a misery whose only utterance is voiceless sighing :—

> "Intent I stood
> To gaze, and in the marish sunk descried
> A miry tribe all naked, and with looks
> Betokening rage. They with their hands alone
> Struck not, but with the head, the breast, the feet,
> Cutting each other piecemeal with their fangs.
>
> . . . . . .
>
> 'This for certain know, that underneath
> The water dwells a multitude, whose sighs
> Into these bubbles make the surface heave,
> As thine eye tells thee wheresoe'er it turn.'"

guilty of a greater, yet it is easy to see that the original tendency of shame is to prevent the doing of shameful actions, and its leading men to conceal such actions when done is only in consequence of their being done, *i.e.* of the passion's not having answered its first end. If it be said that there are persons in the world who are in great measure without the natural affections towards their fellow-creatures, there are likewise instances of persons without the common natural affections to themselves. But the nature of man is not to be judged of by either of these, but what appears in the common world, in the bulk of mankind.

5. Shame. The description of shame given by Novalis illustrates Butler's position : "Shame is a feeling of profanation. Friendship, love, and piety ought to be handled with a sort of mysterious secrecy ; they ought to be spoken of only in the rare moments of perfect confidence, to be mutually understood in silence. Many things are too delicate to be thought, many more to be spoken." The "original tendency" of such a feeling is evidently the prevention of shameful actions. It is intended to guard those things which we are meant to hold most sacred. Suppose, however, that a man's conscience should become so depraved, his pride and self-love so overweening, that he mistakes altogether the nature of true sanctity, and reckons his own security or advantage more sacred than truth or right. Obviously in such a case the sense of shame will be so perverted as to promote what it was intended to prevent. He does wrong ; and shame leads him to conceal the fact, even at the expense of further wrong. He is summoned by every sense of duty to do that which is right, for the doing of which, however, he may be called upon to endure mockery or loss of reputation ; and shame leads him to evade the duty, and side with the mocking world. With shame of this latter sort, every one who has sought the path of duty has been beset. It is this which Bunyan has personified in his great dream, with characteristic insight assigning *Shame* as a special assailant of *Faithful:* "Yes, I met with *Shame;* but of all the men that I met with in my pilgrimage, he, I think, bears the wrong name. The other would be said nay, after a little argumentation (and somewhat else), but this bold-faced *Shame* would never have done. . . . Yea, he did hold me to it . . . that it was a *shame* to sit whining and mourning under a sermon, and a *shame* to come sighing and groaning home ; that it was a *shame* to ask my neighbour forgiveness for petty faults, or to make restitution where I had taken from any. He said also that Religion made a man grow strange to the great, because of a few vices (which he called by finer names), and made him own and respect the base, because of the same Religious Fraternity. And is not this, said he, a shame?"

I am afraid it would be thought very strange [25] if, to confirm the truth of this account of human nature, and make out the justness of the foregoing comparison, it should be added that from what appears, men in fact as much and as often contradict that *part* of their nature which respects *self*, and which leads them to their *own private* good and happiness, as they contradict that *part* of it which respects *society*, and tends to *public* good; that there are as few persons who attain the greatest satisfaction and enjoyment which they might attain in the present world as who do the greatest good to others which they might do; nay, that there are as few who can be said really and in earnest to aim at one as at the other. Take a survey of mankind, the world in general, the good and bad, almost without exception, equally are agreed, that were religion out of the case, the happiness of the present life would consist in a manner wholly in riches, honours, sensual gratifications, insomuch that one scarce hears a reflection made upon prudence, life, conduct, but upon this supposition. Yet, on the contrary, that persons in the greatest affluence of fortune are no happier than such as have only a competency; that the cares and disappointments of ambition for the most part far exceed the satisfactions of it; as also the miserable intervals of intemperance and excess, and the many untimely deaths occasioned by a dissolute course of life; these things are all seen, acknowledged, by every one acknowledged, but are thought no objections against, though they expressly contradict this universal principle, that the happiness of the present life consists in one or other of them.

---

[25] **It would be thought very strange.** This whole paragraph is an *argumentum ad hominem* addressed to those who, both in theory and practice, hold that man is meant to live for private and not for public benefit. You say, he says in effect, that happiness consists in riches, honours, sensual gratifications. Yet it is notorious matter of fact that the pursuit of these things is often fraught with manifold and untold miseries. This you admit; and still you persist in holding that in these things happiness consists. Whence this contradiction? Manifestly, from your not having seriously considered wherein true happiness is to be found, or from your not acting on the result of your consideration. In plain words, passion has prevailed over a calm sense of what is best for you. The inference follows, therefore, that men violate their own best interests as often as those of their fellow-men. The conclusion of the whole matter, accordingly, is that men are meant to pursue the good of others as well as their own. They do not, in either respect, come up to the ideal excellence of life; but this is no proof that in such issues their life was not meant to find its consummation.

Whence is all this absurdity and contradiction? Is not the middle way obvious? Can anything be more manifest than that the happiness of life consists in these, possessed and enjoyed only to a certain degree; that to pursue them beyond this degree is always attended with more inconvenience than advantage to man's self, and often with extreme misery and unhappiness? Whence then, I say, is all this absurdity and contradiction? Is it really the result of consideration in mankind, how they may become most easy to themselves, most free from care, and enjoy the chief happiness attainable in this world? or is it not manifestly owing either to this, that they have not cool and reasonable concern enough for themselves to consider wherein their chief happiness in the present life consists? or else, if they do consider it, that they will not act conformably to what is the result of that consideration? *i.e.* reasonable concern for themselves, or cool self-love, is prevailed over by passion and appetite. So that, from what appears, there is no ground to assert that those principles in the nature of man which most directly lead to promote the good of our fellow-creatures are more generally or in a greater degree violated than those which most directly lead us to promote our own private good and happiness. The sum of the whole is plainly this. The nature of man, considered in his single capacity, and with respect only to the present world, is adapted and leads him to attain the greatest happiness he can for himself in the present world. The nature of man, considered in his public or social capacity, leads him to a right behaviour in society, to that course of life which we call virtue. Men follow or obey their nature in both these capacities and respects to a certain degree, but not entirely; their actions do not come up to the whole of what their nature leads them to in either of these capacities or respects, and they often violate their nature in both; *i.e.* as they neglect the duties they owe to their fellow-creatures, to which their nature leads them, and are injurious, to which their nature is abhorrent, so there is a manifest negligence in men of their real happiness or interest in the present world, when that interest is inconsistent with a present gratification for the sake of which they negligently, nay, even knowingly, are the authors and instruments of their own misery and ruin. Thus they are as often unjust to themselves as to others, and for the most part are equally so to both by the same actions.

SERMON II.

UPON HUMAN NATURE.

"For when the Gentiles, which have not the law, do by nature the things contained in the law, these, having not the law, are a law unto themselves."—ROM. ii. 14.

AS speculative truth admits of different kinds of proof, so likewise moral obligations may be shown by different methods. If the real nature of any creature leads him, and is adapted to such and such purposes only, or more than to any other; this is a reason to believe the author of that nature intended it for those purposes. Thus there is no doubt the eye was intended for us to see with.[1] And the more complex any

---

[1] **The eye was intended for us to see with.** Butler here makes use, for purposes of ethical study, of the argument from design, whose ordinary application is in the field of theology, to demonstrate the being of a God. In the preface he has used the illustration of a watch, from the relations of whose parts fitly arranged we gather that its end is to mark time. So, he argues, observe the parts which constitute human nature, and you shall learn what is the chief end of man. Butler is perfectly confident of the success of his method, though he points out in the sequel some of its difficulties. A later age has not been quite so assured. It has been informed by modern physical and sociological science of so many things which seem to throw doubt on the presence of design and a Designer, that it holds somewhat timidly the faith that "good will be the final goal of ill." The truth is that in our study both of the world and of man, the end we seek to reach must be in a certain sense our starting-point. The "far-off divine event" must be present all through to our thought, else we shall never be able to justify to ourselves the belief that to it "the whole creation moves." We must know God, if we are ever to know nature or man. God is not the conclusion of a syllogism, but the necessary presupposition as well of knowing as of being. "Know thyself" is an old and venerable moral precept. When, however, we seek to know ourselves, we find that we are forced beyond ourselves to Another who is the

constitution is, and the greater variety of parts there are, which thus tend to some end, the stronger is the proof that such end was designed. However, when the inward frame of man is considered as any guide in morals, the utmost caution[2] must be used, that none make peculiarities in their own temper, or anything

---

source and interpretation of our whole being. Only when we know Him can we understand the true end of human nature; only thus can we see how all the "variety of parts" which exists within us is welded into a perfect spiritual unity. As it is within ourselves, so is it with the wider world of which we are parts. The varied elements in it are elements of an organic whole, and only from this point of view can they be understood, and their mutual relations adjusted. The world is intelligible only from a point of view which shows us at the same time that it is a world in which good is triumphant.

[2] *The utmost caution.* The difficulties in the way of self-knowledge are indeed great. Two things, Butler mentions, have to be guarded against; mistaking the peculiarity of an individual or the custom of a class for a characteristic quality of man as such; and omitting the principle which regulates every other element in man's nature. So many differences exist in regard to the nature of the moral sense, and such close and careful scrutiny is required in studying human nature, that the work of introspection is made exceedingly complicated and delicate. Difficulties like these have thrown discredit on the whole process of self-knowledge, and have sent Carlyle into a characteristic paradox of contradiction. "The latest gospel in this world is, know thy work and do it. 'Know thyself;' long enough has that poor 'self' of thine tormented thee; thou wilt never get to 'know' it, I believe! Think it not thy business, this of knowing thyself; thou art an unknowable individual: know what thou canst work at, and work at it like a Hercules! That will be thy better plan." It is true that self cannot be known where it is held apart in unreal isolation. It can be known only through and in the moral and spiritual realm of which it is an integral part. But it *is* known in this way. It is not lost or absorbed in the immensity of the whole. In God we find ourselves and know ourselves; and any effort to ignore self or proceed without self-knowledge will lead to intellectual error and moral shipwreck. The ultimate good is a good in which *we* have a part, and of which *we* must possess ourselves. The individualism which concentrates all interest on the "self," the reaction from individualism which attempts to ignore the self and deny its claims, are alike one-sided and false. There is a "more excellent way" than either. This is seen in actual fact amid the numbers of those who, in unknown heroism and lowly self-sacrifice, have lost their lives and so truly found them. We need a philosophy which shall be adequate to the rich fulness of this fact. The terms "self," "individual," "person," await fuller discussion and more perfect comprehension.

which is the effect of particular customs, though observable in several, the standard of what is common to the species; and, above all, that the highest principle be not forgot or excluded, that to which belongs the adjustment and correction of all other inward movements and affections; which principle will, of course, have some influence, but which, being in nature supreme, as shall now be shown, ought to preside over and govern all the rest. The difficulty of rightly observing the two former cautions, the appearance there is of some small diversity amongst mankind with respect to this faculty, with respect to their natural sense of moral good and evil, and the attention necessary to survey with any exactness what passes within, have occasioned that it is not so much agreed what is the standard of the internal nature of man, as of his external form. Neither is this last exactly settled. Yet we understand one another when we speak of the shape of a human body; so likewise we do when we speak of the heart and inward principles,[3] how far soever the standard is from being exact or precisely fixed. There is therefore ground for an attempt of showing men to themselves,—of showing them what course of life and behaviour their real nature points out, and would lead them to. Now, obligations of virtue shown, and motives to the practice of it enforced, from a review of the nature of man, are to be considered as an appeal to each particular person's heart and natural conscience; as the external senses

---

[3] **The heart and inward principles.** Butler's argument is that, from what man *is*, we may learn what he is *meant to be.* He insists that, spite of the difficulties which attend self-knowledge, it is possible to attain a generally trustworthy estimate of "the heart and inward principles." Thus "showing men to themselves," we may address their "natural conscience" with convincing persuasion in favour of virtue. The converse of this position is, however, the higher truth. We learn what man *is* from consideration of what he is *meant to be.* We contemplate the good to which he is meant to attain, and with which he is meant to be identified; and thus we discover the meaning and purpose of the varied elements of his nature. We "show men to themselves" most truly when we present to them the picture of that perfect humanity which was revealed in the man Christ Jesus. This, the presentation of the manhood of Christ, is the mightiest appeal which can be addressed to the conscience, for, seeing Christ, men see at once what they were meant to be, and what they are in comparison with this standard, and are moved to imitation by the sense that this is their true self. Nay, by His Spirit they *become* what they *truly* are.

SERMON II.—UPON HUMAN NATURE.

are appealed to for the proof of things cognizable by them. Since, then, our inward feelings, and the perceptions we receive from our external senses, are equally real, to argue from the former to life and conduct is as little liable to exception, as to argue from the latter to absolute speculative truth. A man can as little doubt whether his eyes were given him to see with, as he can doubt of the truth of the science of *optics*, deduced from ocular experiments. And allowing the inward feeling, shame, a man can as little doubt whether it was given him to prevent his doing shameful actions, as he can doubt whether his eyes were given him to guide his steps. And as to these inward feelings themselves; that they are real—that man has in his nature passions and affections, can no more be questioned than that he has external senses. Neither can the former be wholly mistaken, though to a certain degree liable to greater mistakes than the latter.

There can be no doubt but that several propensions or instincts, several principles in the heart of man, carry him to society, and to contribute to the happiness of it, in a sense and a manner in which no inward principle leads him to evil. These principles, propensions, or instincts, which lead him to do good, are approved of by a certain faculty within, quite distinct from these propensions themselves. All this hath been fully made out in the foregoing discourse.

But it may be said, What is all this, though true, to the purpose of virtue and religion?[4] These require not only that we

---

[4] **Virtue and religion.** Butler supposes himself to be now confronted with a serious objection. The supposed opponent argues thus: You have indeed proved that man has instincts which lead him to do good to his fellows. You have even proved that he has a conscience. With all this, however, you have failed to lay a firm basis for morality or religion. These require, not only that man should have certain principles which may at times be stronger than others, but that his *whole* character should be *always* under the control of some determinate rule. As far, therefore, as the mere possession of certain instincts goes, even with conscience superadded, it does not appear that man is one whit different from the brutes. They follow their strongest impulse, and so act according to the nature which God has given them. Man obeys his strongest impulse, be it passion or conscience, and in either case he, too, is acting according to his nature, and is fulfilling the end of his existence. This is the kind of language which vice borrowed from the prevailing philosophy of the day in order to gain for itself some sort of justification. If the view of

do good to others when we are led this way, by benevolence or reflection happening to be stronger than other principles, passions, or appetites; but likewise that the *whole* character be formed upon thought and reflection; that *every* action be directed by some determinate rule, some other rule than the strength and prevalence of any principle or passion. What sign is there in our nature (for the inquiry is only about what is to be collected from thence) that this was intended by its Author? or how does so various and fickle a temper as that of man appear adapted thereto? It may indeed be absurd and unnatural for men to act without any reflection; nay, without regard to that particular kind of reflection which you call conscience; because this does belong to our nature. For, as there never was a man but who approved one place, prospect, building, before another, so does it not appear that there ever was a man who would not have approved an action of humanity rather than of cruelty; interest and passion being quite out of the case. But interest and passion do come in, and are often too strong for, and prevail over, reflection and conscience. Now, as brutes

---

human nature taken by some philosophers be true, and man's primary instincts are for sensual gratification, the practical inference can only be, let him by all means gratify himself. The restraints which society puts upon him are purely artificial, and their disregard involves no fault. If, indeed, there are such instincts as benevolence, or if there be such a thing as conscience, let those follow them who list; but let not such persons blame those who follow other equally natural tendencies. The type of philosophizing to which this language most nearly approximates is that of Bernard de Mandeville, whose *Fable of the Bees* was published in 1723. His view was that men had no motive powers save their passions; that morality is an artificial product, the invention of clever persons who for their own private ends conspired to induce men to give up their self-interest, and submit to the yoke imposed on them. The instrument of persuasion was flattery, and thus "the moral virtues are the political offspring which flattery begot upon pride." Butler replies to this strain of argument, that it implies that men follow nature as much when they yield to the promptings of desire as when, in obedience to a different impulse, they conquer them. If "nature" mean merely what pleases us, then in a sense, of course, we always follow nature. In this sense, however, the phrase would have no ethical significance. The whole difficulty will be met by considering the various senses in which "nature" is to be understood. This will bring out the true meaning of the phrase when it is sought to establish it as the guide of life, "that by which men are a guide to themselves."

have various instincts by which they are carried on to the end the Author of their nature intended them for, is not man in the same condition, with this difference only, that to his instincts (*i.e.* appetites and passions) is added the principle of reflection or conscience? And as brutes act agreeably to their nature, in following that principle, a particular instinct, which for the present is strongest in them; does not man likewise act agreeably to his nature, or obey the law of his creation, by following that principle, be it passion or conscience, which for the present happens to be strongest in him? Thus, different men are by their particular nature hurried on to pursue honour, or riches, or pleasure; there are also persons whose temper leads them in an uncommon degree to kindness, compassion, doing good to their fellow-creatures; as there are others who are given to suspend their judgment, to weigh and consider things, and to act upon thought and reflection. Let every one then quietly follow his nature; as passion, reflection, appetite, the several parts of it, happen to be the strongest; but let not the man of virtue take upon him to blame the ambitious, the covetous, the dissolute; since these, equally with him, obey and follow their nature. Thus, as in some cases, we follow our nature in doing the works *contained in the law;* so, in other cases, we follow our nature in doing contrary. Now all this licentious talk entirely goes upon a supposition, that men follow their nature, in the same sense, in violating the known rules of justice and honesty for the sake of a present gratification, as they do in following those rules when they have no temptation to the contrary. And if this were true, that could not be so which St. Paul asserts, that men are "by nature a law to themselves." If by following nature were meant only acting as we please, it would indeed be ridiculous to speak of nature as any guide in morals: nay, the very mention of deviating from nature would be absurd; and the mention of following it, when spoken by way of distinction, would absolutely have no meaning. For, did ever any one act otherwise than as he pleased? And yet the ancients speak of deviating from nature as vice; and of following nature[5] so much as a distinction, that, according to them, the

---

[5] **Following nature.** The "ancients" whose ethical teaching was summed up in the precept "Follow nature" were the Greek Stoics; and Butler, endorsing as he does their teaching on this point, is a Stoic among British moralists. The founder of the Stoic school was Zeno, who was born about 340 B.C. His immediate successors were

perfection of virtue consists therein. So that language itself should teach people another sense to the words *following nature,*

Cleanthes and Chrysippus, the latter of whom died about 208 B.C. The philosophy of Aristotle had regarded the world as constituted by two elements, mind, νοῦς, and matter, ὕλη. Aristotle had not been able to indicate any point of view from which these two principles might be seen to express a deeper unity. It remained, accordingly, for later thinkers who were dissatisfied with the Aristotelian partition of the world into two parts or elements, to adopt one or other of these principles, and make it supreme. The Stoics chose the former, the spiritual principle; the Epicureans the latter, the material principle. The Stoics held the world to be a vast living body of which God is the life or rational soul. Of this great whole, man is a part. His true nature is that reason which animates and regulates the world. From this view of man follows their great ethical principle, "Follow nature," or "live in agreement with nature," or more particularly, "Follow thine own rational nature; make reason, which is thy true nature, thy guide; and follow not thine own selfish desire, which is indeed unreason." Hence, according to the Stoics, as Butler says, "the perfection of virtue consists" in following nature. Stoicism proved an immense practical power in the ancient world. When the imperial despotisms of Alexander, and later of Rome, broke up the ancient civic life in which a high degree of moral development had been possible, men required a refuge in which their souls might be secure from the oppression and dissatisfaction of a world where they were now no longer free, but the bond-slaves of an iron will. Stoicism proclaimed Reason as such a refuge. In obeying reason, man was made master of his fate, competent to defy all the ills of the world. Beyond the individual characters which Stoicism made strong and brave, results of quite unspeakable value for the future of civilisation were secured by the entrance of Stoic principles into the domain of law. If the true worth of man be not the outward circumstance of birth or rank, but his personality as a rational being, then every man has the same value through the principle of reason which is common to all. Thus was established the great principle of the value of man as such, which Christianity appropriated and vivified, by which slavery has been crushed and tyranny overcome, and which is to-day winning fresh triumphs in the enfranchisement of the poorest and the humblest. Stoicism, considered as a general attitude of soul, has been strongest, as well as most valuable, where institutions in which men once found satisfaction have been destroyed, and in their place has come a time of despotism or of anarchy. Then the individual retreating into the citadel of his own spirit has been strong to defy the world even when it crushed him. Thus the mediæval mystics sought refuge in individual communion with infinite Light and Love from the tyranny of Rome. This also is the gospel which Butler preaches to a

than barely acting as we please. Let it, however, be observed, though the words *human nature* are to be explained, yet the real question of this discourse is not concerning the meaning of the words, any otherwise than as the explanation of them may be needful to make out and explain the assertion, *that every man is naturally a law to himself, that every one may find within himself the rule of right, and obligations to follow it.* This St. Paul affirms in the words of the text, and this the foregoing objection really denies, by seeming to allow it. And the objection will be fully answered, and the text before us explained, by observing, that *nature* is considered in different views, and the word used in different senses; and by showing in what view it is considered, and in what sense the word is used, when intended to express and signify that which is the guide of life, that by which men are a law to themselves. I say, the explanation of the term [c]

---

disorganized society where virtue and religion were openly derided. Obey nature, he cries, thine own true constitution, and thus rise superior to the solicitations of desire, the importunity or persecution of the world, the delusions and enthusiastic dreamings of superstition.

[c] **The explanation of the term.** Proceeding now to discuss the term nature, Butler notices three senses in which it may be understood. I. "Some principle in man without regard either to the kind or degree of it." In this use of the term no moral quality is implied. In this sense nature cannot be that by which we are a guide to ourselves. Our nature in this aspect is simply the instinctive basis of character that is beneath moral qualification. In ordinary language, however, we do sometimes impart into the phrase some moral estimate. Thus we employ it in excuse or in approbation; "it was but natural he should act in such a manner," "he acted naturally and unaffectedly." II. "Those passions which are strongest and most influence the actions." Butler's account of man as "vicious by nature" is given from the non-theological, natural history standpoint, which he never abandons in these three sermons. As a mere matter of observation, therefore, he points out that the passions which are strongest are vicious. His use of Scripture, accordingly, is scarcely in accordance with sound interpretation. In the passage which he quotes much more is meant than the mere observation that men's strongest passions are vicious. The New Testament uses language with respect to man which justifies the strongest statements of theology as to the corruption of man's whole nature; and these statements will not be resented by those who know the disease of their own hearts. Scripture and experience, therefore, concur in describing man as by nature sinful. Both alike, however, assert that this is not man's true nature. His perfect manhood is in Christ; he is himself

will be sufficient, because from thence it will appear that, in some senses of the word nature cannot be, but that in another sense it manifestly is, a law to us.

---

when he is like Him. To speak of man as naturally sinful does not therefore imply any excuse for his being so, as though it were his nature, and he could not help it; but really conveys a tremendous moral censure. This indeed is your nature; but it is yours only to be crucified, that, through the death of nature, you may reach that nature which is yours in another, and in which for the first time you attain your true nature. So long, therefore, as you remain in sin, you are not only dishonouring God and His law, you are desecrating the glory of your true being. III. "The Gentiles do by nature the things contained in the law." Butler thus finds a scriptural authority for that particular sense of "nature" in which it is a moral guide. The New Testament indicates three stages in man's realization of goodness or righteousness. 1. Nature. At this stage the Gentiles stand. Goodness here appears as impulse, rising within the heart of man with a force and authority that remain unquestioned. Man does not hold himself apart from this impulse, to criticize it, and then deliberately to accept and follow it. He *knows* nothing about it. He only *feels* it, and acts on its inspiration. There is a singular beauty in such virtue. It is unquestioning as a child's, and the breath of thought has not dimmed the clear surface in which we see fair images of truth, and love, and constancy. Thus also it is occasional, incidental, passing into act at the call of some special instinct. Antigone represents the almighty instinct of *family love*, when in opposition to the authority of the State she performs in tears the sacred rites over the body of her brother, appealing as she does so to a law higher than that of the State, unwritten yet eternal:

> "It is not of to-day, nor yesterday,
> It lives for ever, none knows whence it is."

Achilles and Patroclus, Orestes and Pylades, Damon and Pythias, are examples of the love which raises the *friendship* of antiquity almost to an equality, in respect of faithfulness and devotion, with marriage under Christian influence. The *love of country* awakes in the citizen's heart as a capacity of infinite sacrifice; and for this sacred cause he can face with Leonidas mighty odds and inevitable death, or perish with Regulus amid unspeakable tortures. Such things, contained in the Law, the Gentiles do by Nature. The question here arises as to the relation of this statement to that which Butler has just quoted, that men are "by nature children of wrath." How can men do *by nature* the things contained in the Law, and yet be *by nature* children of wrath? The difficulty has been solved by saying that "the virtues of the heathen are splendid vices,"

I. By nature is often meant no more than some principle in man, without regard either to the kind or degree of it. Thus the passion of anger, and the affection of parents to their children, would be called equally natural. And as the same person hath often contrary principles, which at the same time draw contrary ways, he may by the same action both follow and contradict his nature in this sense of the word; he may follow one passion and contradict another.

II. Nature is frequently spoken of as consisting in those passions which are strongest, and most influence the actions; which being vicious ones, mankind is in this sense naturally vicious, or vicious by nature. Thus St. Paul says of the Gentiles, *who were dead in trespasses and sins, and walked according to the*

---

and so depriving them of all moral value. In this statement, however, it is presupposed that good works are the ground of man's acceptance with God. Then, with respect to those who are not accepted, it follows as a logical consequence that they can have no good works, and what appear to be so must be regarded as *splendida vitia*. The truth is, that men stand to God in a twofold relation by nature. (1) They are made in His image, meant for His service, designed for His fellowship, in which alone they can find true satisfaction. But they have debased that image, declined that service, despised that fellowship. Thus they have lost the perfection of their own being, and abide now "under His wrath and curse." Such are all men "by nature." (2) They are His children, never cast off, loved with the infinite passion of a God who is also Father. Their years are spent under His providence and His discipline. The instincts of family, friendship, country, and all other impulses after righteousness, are part of the revelation in them and to them of the good for which He has created them, some of the means by which He seeks to bring them thither. Their deeds of devotion, heroism, etc., they do, accordingly, "by nature," which is only another name for the mercy of the Father, who thus gathers His lost children to Himself. The virtues of the heathen are not meritorious, but they are not on that account valueless. No good works have the value of merit with God. All virtues, in Gentile and Christian alike, are the consequence of a Witness to the Good, and a Power of seeking it, which the Father withholds from none of His children. 2. Law. Natural virtues we have described as instinctive in their motive and incidental in their exercise. In the transition from Nature to Law these characteristics are left behind. The *motive* of moral conduct is now obedience to an authority imposed from without. There is lost, accordingly, the spontaneity and freedom which makes natural goodness so beautiful; while there is gained that sense of

spirit of disobedience, that *they were by nature the children of wrath* (Eph. ii. 3). They could be no otherwise *children of wrath* by nature, than they were vicious by nature.

Here then are two different senses of the word *nature*, in neither of which men can at all be said to be a law to themselves. They are mentioned only to be excluded; to prevent their being confounded, as the latter is in the objection, with another sense of it, which is now to be inquired after and explained.

III. The apostle asserts, that the Gentiles *do by nature the things contained in the law.* Nature is indeed here put by way of distinction from revelation, but yet it is not a mere negative. He intends to express more than that by which they *did not* than by which they *did* the works of the law, namely, by nature.

---

personal obligation to the claim of righteousness which is the condition of moral growth. The *exercise* of virtue becomes now systematic. Righteousness is not left to occasional incidents to suggest its exercise. It lays its grasp upon the whole of life, and seeks to bring every action under some detailed obligation. There awakens, accordingly, the sense of sin, of trespass upon obligation, which is wholly absent from the era of natural goodness. Along with this, the sense of the infinitude of the Law's demands, and the utter incapacity of man to comply with them, deepens in every earnest soul; and Law breeds a despair which requires a gospel to redeem it from moral death. 3. Grace. The sunshine of nature has passed through gloomy shades of Law to emerge now in a clearer and sweeter light. The infinite inaccessibility of righteousness disappears. It is brought near to man, "closer than breathing, nearer than hands or feet." It is the quality of the new life upon which through death he has entered. It is his, not by imputation alone, but as the energy of his being, in Christ who is his life. The righteousness of grace, therefore, gathers into itself the qualities of both previous stages. It fulfils the righteousness of the law, but in doing so it preserves those features which gave beauty to natural virtue. Its *motive* is not obedience to external authority, but the upspringing of an inner fountain of love rising toward that source of good from whence it came, seeking with the intensity of personal devotion the glory of the Christ who first evoked it. It therefore retains the spontaneity and freedom of nature. It is, in fact, nature born again. Its *exercise* is not adherence to a system of rules, however elaborate or complete, but the ceaseless outgoing of a power which, under all the circumstances and amid all the emergencies of this complex human life, endeavours to do the will of God and establish that kingdom which is righteousness, and peace, and

It is plain the meaning of the word is not the same in this passage as in the former, where it is spoken of as evil; for in the latter it is spoken of as good; as that by which they acted, or might have acted virtuously. What that is in man by which he is *naturally a law to himself*,[7] is explained in the following words: *which shows the work of the law written in their hearts, their consciences also bearing witness, and their thoughts the meanwhile accusing or else excusing one another.* If there be a distinction to be made between the *works written in their hearts* and the *witness of conscience*, by the former must be meant the natural disposition to kindness and compassion, to do what is of good report, to which the apostle often refers; that part of the nature of man, treated of in the foregoing discourse, which, with very little reflection and of course, leads him to society, and by

---

joy. It has lost, accordingly, all tinge of the Pharisaic spirit wellnigh inseparable from life under law. It makes no professions, but continually, as every incident of life forms occasion, it performs without ostentation the will with which it is altogether one. Paul's spiritual biography illustrates what has just been said. First, he lives a life of natural unconscious goodness. "I was alive without the law once." Then he falls under the bondage of law. "When the commandment came, sin revived, and I died." The horrors of the situation, in which goodness remained unattainable, and how to perform that which was good he found not, he paints in dark colours. Finally came that dark hour, which, however, by God's mercy, preceded the dawn. "O wretched man that I am! who shall deliver me from the body of this death? I thank God through Jesus Christ our Lord." And now, possessing a life whose features are "no condemnation," "the Spirit dwelling in us," "the spirit of adoption," he stands forth more than a conqueror, and is persuaded of his inalienable inheritance in the love of God which is in Christ Jesus our Lord (see Rom. vii. and viii. *passim*).

[7] **Naturally a law to himself.** Having dismissed the two previous meanings, Butler now seeks to establish the correct interpretation of nature, according to which it may be taken as the guide of life. In the text which he quotes, "Nature" is analysed into "*works written in their hearts*," and "the *witness of conscience.*" The former Butler identifies with merely natural impulses to goodness. But as some natural impulses tend, though indirectly, to evil, and as we cannot determine the proportion in which these two kinds of impulses stand to one another, we cannot from them derive the guide of life. There remains, accordingly, the witness of conscience. To live according to nature, therefore, is to live according to conscience. In this sense of the term man is a law to himself.

means of which he naturally acts a just and good part in it, unless other passions or interests lead him astray. Yet since other passions and regards to private interest, which lead us (though indirectly, yet lead us) astray, are themselves in a degree equally natural, and often most prevalent; and since we have no method of seeing the particular degrees in which one or the other is placed in us by nature, it is plain the former, considered merely as natural, good and right as they are, can no more be a law to us than the latter. But there is a superior principle of reflection or conscience in every man; which distinguishes between the internal principles of his heart, as well as his external actions; which passes judgment upon himself and them; pronounces determinately some actions to be in themselves just, right, good; others to be in themselves evil, wrong, unjust; which, without being consulted, without being advised with, magisterially exerts itself,[8] and approves or condemns him, the doer of them, accordingly; and which, if not forcibly stopped, naturally and always, of course, goes on to anticipate a higher and more effectual sentence,[9] which shall hereafter second and affirm

---

[8] **Magisterially exerts itself.** The figure of the court-room as applied to conscience is familiar in literature. Every man bears about

> "A silent court of justice in his breast,
> Himself the judge and jury, and himself
> The prisoner at the bar, ever condemned;
> And that drags down his life."
>
> TENNYSON, *Sea Dreams.*

> "But 't is not so above;
> There is no shuffling, there the action lies
> In his true nature; and we ourselves compell'd
> Even to the teeth and forehead of our faults,
> To give in evidence."
>
> *Hamlet*, Act iii. Scene 3.

> "My conscience hath a thousand several tongues,
> And every tongue brings in a several tale,
> And every tale condemns me for a villain.
> Perjury, perjury, in the high'st degree,
> Murder, stern murder, in the direst degree;
> All several sins, all used in each degree,
> Throng to the bar, crying all,—Guilty! Guilty!"
>
> *K. Richard III.*, Act v. Scene 3.

[9] **A higher and more effectual sentence.** "View the conscience and thoughts, with their self-reflecting abilities, wherein the soul retires into itself, and sits concealed from all eyes but His that made it, judging its own actions and censuring its estate; viewing its face in

its own. But this part of the office of conscience is beyond my present design explicitly to consider. It is by this faculty natural to man that he is a moral agent, that he is a law to himself: by this faculty, I say, not to be considered merely as a principle in his heart which is to have some influence as well as others; but considered as a faculty, in kind and in nature, supreme over all others, and which bears its own authority of being so.

This *prerogative*, this *natural supremacy*,[10] of the faculty which

---

its own glass, and correcting the indecencies it discovers there. Things of greatest moment and importance are silently transacted in its council chamber betwixt the soul and God. Here it impleads, condemns, and acquits itself as at a privy session, with respect to the judgment of the great day: here it meets with the best of comforts, and with the worst of terrors."—Flavel. "Conscience is the judgment of man upon himself, as he is subject to the judgment of God. ... Conscience, therefore, is a high and awful power, it is *solo Deo minor;* next, and immediately under God our Judge; riding, as Joseph did, in the second chariot. ... Its consolations are of all the most sweet, and its condemnations (only excepting those by the mouth of Christ in the last judgment) most terrible. ... Wherever you go, conscience accompanies you; whatever you say, do, or but think, it registers and records, in order to the day of account. When all friends forsake thee, yea, when thy soul forsakes thy body, conscience will not, cannot forsake thee. When thy body is weakest and dullest, thy conscience is most vigorous and active. Never more life in the conscience than when death makes its nearest approach to the body. When it smiles, cheers, acquits, and comforts, oh, what a heaven doth it create within a man! And when it frowns, condemns, and terrifies, how doth it becloud, yea, benight all the pleasures, joy, and delights of this world! ... It is certainly the best of friends, or the worst of enemies in the whole creation."—Flavel.

"When a man has done any villainous act, though under countenance of the highest place and power, and under covert of the closest secrecy, his conscience, for all that, strikes him like a clap of thunder, and depresses him to a perpetual trepidation, horror, and poorness of spirit. ... And all this because he has heard a condemning sentence from within, which the secret forebodings of his mind tell him will be ratified by a sad and certain execution from above: on the other side, what makes a man so cheerful, so bright and confident in his comforts, but because he finds himself acquitted by God's high commissioner and deputy?"—South.

[10] **This prerogative, this natural supremacy.** Having thus shown the true idea of nature, and having exhibited the function of conscience though without entering into details, Butler devotes the rest of this

surveys, approves, or disapproves the several affections of our mind and actions of our lives, being that by which men *are a law to themselves*, their conformity or disobedience to which law of our nature renders their actions, in the highest and most proper sense, natural or unnatural; it is fit it be further explained to you: and I hope it will be so, if you will attend to the following reflections.

Man may act [11] according to that principle or inclination which for the present happens to be strongest, and yet act in a way disproportionate to, and violate his real proper nature. Suppose a brute creature, by any bait, to be allured into a snare by which he is destroyed, he plainly followed the bent of his nature,

---

sermon to vindicating the authority or natural supremacy of conscience. His argument is elaborated with redundant care.

[11] (1.) **Man may act.** The first stage of the argument establishes the distinction between man and the brutes with respect to instinctive action. A brute always follows its instincts, and in so doing is acting according to its natural constitution, even when the consequences of the action are fatal to itself. A man, however, who should gratify a strong impulse, in reckless disregard of consequences, is acting in an utterly unnatural way, for the mere impulse, however strong, is a wholly subordinate part of human nature, and to obey it, therefore, is to introduce disproportion and disharmony into the whole of life and character.

Probably the truest notion we can form of the life of one of the lower animals is that it is governed by a number of blind impulses, which are never brought by the animal itself into the focus of one all-embracing end or purpose, though in the case of some of the higher domestic animals an external and artificial unity is given to the life through subjection to the authority of a master. It is equally natural, therefore, for the animal to follow any one of these impulses in any direction whatever. It is sometimes discussed whether there are in man any instincts properly so called. However that may be, the distinguishing characteristic of man is his faculty of comprehending the various tendencies and impulses of his being in their relation to some end in the attainment of which his true nature is satisfied. For him, therefore, to follow an impulse because it happened to be strong, without considering its bearing upon the end of life, would be in the highest degree unnatural and wrong. Consciousness of an end in view is thus the distinction between instinctive and non-moral and rational and moral action. "The fundamental difference," according to Martineau, *Types of Ethical Theory*, vol. ii. p. 139, is "that human habit sets agoing the instrumental links of *an end in view;* while animal instinct institutes and follows out the means to an end which is *out of view.*"

leading him to gratify his appetite; there is an entire correspondence between his whole nature and such an action; such action therefore is natural. But suppose a man, foreseeing the same danger of certain ruin, should rush into it for the sake of a present gratification; he in this instance would follow his strongest desire, as did the brute creature, but there would be as manifest a disproportion between the nature of man and such an action, as between the meanest work of art and the skill of the greatest master in that art; which disproportion arises, not from considering the action singly in *itself*, or in its *consequences*, but from the *comparison* of it with the nature of the agent. And since such an action is utterly disproportionate to the nature of man, it is in the strictest and most proper sense unnatural; this word expressing that disproportion. Therefore, instead of the words *disproportionate to his nature*, the word *unnatural* may now be put, this being more familiar to us; but let it be observed, that it stands for the same thing precisely.

Now, what is it [12] which renders such a rash action unnatural? Is it that he went against the principle of reasonable and cool self-love, considered *merely* as a part of his nature? No; for if he had acted the contrary way, he would equally have gone

---

[12] (2.) Now, what is it. In the second place, on comparing some particular instinct with the general principle of self-love, we are led to see that the difference between them does not lie in the degree of strength possessed by each. The difference lies in the fact that the principle of self-love is in nature and kind superior to any mere passion. Accordingly, to thwart a passion under the guidance of enlightened self-love is right and rational; while to defy self-love at the dictate of some passion is to upset the whole constitution of human nature. Thus there is established a difference of kind among the parts of human nature.

The exhibition of vice as unnatural, being, so to speak, the madness of human nature, constitutes a mighty dissuasive from it. It is indeed not the highest ground which may be taken; and if it were used in a merely selfish interest, as who should say, "Don't do that, or it will be the worse for you," it would be an immoral argument in favour of morality. But if we regard morality as the achievement of the highest end for which human nature is adapted, then it is fair to stimulate men to abandon certain courses of action by pointing out their consequences for time and for eternity. The Bible uses this argument, though sparingly. It warns men that "he that soweth to the flesh shall of the flesh reap corruption;" and it entreats men to "flee from the wrath to come." Writers who do not stand at the Christian point of view, or who desire to appeal to those who would decline the

against a principle or part of his nature, namely, passion or appetite. But to deny a present appetite from foresight that the gratification of it would end in immediate ruin or extreme misery, is by no means an unnatural action; whereas to contradict or go against cool self-love for the sake of such gratification is so in the instance before us. Such an action, then, being unnatural, and its being so not arising from a man's going against that principle or desire barely, nor in going against that principle or desire which happens for the present to be strongest; it necessarily follows that there must be some other difference or distinction to be made between these two principles, passion and cool self-love, than what I have yet taken notice of. And this difference, not being a difference in strength or degree, I call a difference in *nature* and in *kind*. And since, in the instance still before us, if passion prevails over self-love, the consequent action is unnatural; but if self-love prevails over passion, the action is natural; it is manifest that self-love is in human nature a superior principle to passion. This may be contradicted without violating that nature, but the former cannot. So that, if we will act conformably to the economy of man's nature, reasonable self-love must govern. Thus, without particular consideration of conscience, we may have a clear conception of the *superior nature* of one inward principle to another; and see that there really is this natural superiority, quite distinct

---

highest arguments, have eloquently asserted the unnaturalness and misery of vice,—

> "The gods are just, and of our pleasant vices
> Make instruments to scourge us."
> *King Lear*, Act v. Scene 2.

> "The expense of spirit in a waste of shame
> Is lust in action; and till action, lust
> Is perjur'd, murderous, bloody, full of blame,
> Savage, extreme, rude, cruel, not to trust;
> Enjoy'd no sooner but despised straight;
> Past reason hunted; and no sooner had,
> Past reason hated, as the swallow'd bait,
> On purpose laid to make the taker mad:
> Mad in pursuit, and in possession so;
> Had, having, and in quest to have, extreme;
> A bliss in proof,—and proved, a very woe;
> Before, a joy propos'd; behind, a dream.
> All this the world well knows; yet none knows well
> To shun the heaven that leads men to this hell."
> SHAKESPEARE'S *Sonnets*, No. 129.

from degrees of strength and prevalency. Let us now take a view [13] of the nature of man as consisting partly of various appetites, passions, affections, and partly of the principle of reflection, or conscience, leaving quite out all consideration of the different degrees of strength in which either of them prevail; and it will further appear that there is this natural superiority of one inward principle to another, or that it is even part of the idea of reflection or conscience. Passion or appetite implies a direct simple tendency towards such and such objects without distinction of the means by which they are to be obtained. Consequently, it will often happen there will be a desire of particular

---

[13] (3.) Let us now take a view. In the case of passion and self-love, it has been seen that self-love has a natural superiority over passion. Now, in the third place, take conscience, and it will be seen to be gifted with this characteristic of superiority, and to be supreme over every other part of human nature. Passion, for instance, leads us to conduct which involves injury to others. Conscience imperiously forbids us to follow this leading. It claims to be obeyed, not because it is stronger as an impulse, but because it is endowed with a superior authority. If passion prevails, it will be because it has usurped a position which does not belong to it. In a civil State, mere power must bow to rightful authority. So in the state and constitution of man, conscience bears sway, not by its power, but by its natural authority. This indeed is its peculiarity, that it occupies a position of such supremacy that, if it had power to enforce its decisions, it would be master of the world.

The figure which Butler here presents to us is that of a State or a kingdom. Its lawful head is conscience, which is naturally and rightfully supreme over every department of the State. Its decisions are law for the community of impulses and desires over which it presides. While thus strong, nay almighty, as a judicial authority, Conscience is unfortunately very weak in the executive department, nay, it possesses no executive powers whatever. Subject to Conscience, are the passions and appetites which possess just that quality of strength which conscience lacks. It occasionally happens, therefore, that the passions and appetites make head against the decrees of Conscience, and, by dint of mere force, thrust themselves into a position of supremacy,—

"And the state of man,
Like to a little kingdom, suffers then
The nature of an insurrection."

Destitute though Conscience be of force, however, it is not therefore a *roi fainéant*. It bears sway throughout the moral world by virtue

objects, in cases where they cannot be obtained without manifest injury to others, reflection or conscience comes in and disapproves the pursuit of them in these circumstances, but the desire re-

---

of its inherent right, and through its decree order and harmony prevail.

> "Stern daughter of the voice of God!
> O Duty! If that name thou love
> Who art a light to guide, a rod
> To check the erring, and reprove;
> Thou who art victory and law
> When empty terrors overawe;
> From vain temptations dost set free,
> And calm'st the weary strife of frail humanity!
>
> . . . . .
>
> Stern Lawgiver! yet thou dost wear
> The Godhead's most benignant grace;
> Nor know we anything so fair
> As is the smile upon thy face:
> Flowers laugh before thee on their beds,
> And fragrance in thy footing treads;
> Thou dost preserve the stars from wrong;
> And the most ancient heavens, through Thee, are fresh and strong."
>   WORDSWORTH'S *Ode to Duty.*

And though it may have no power of its own, yet no power on earth can control it. "This vicegerent of God has one prerogative above all God's other earthly vicegerents; to wit, that it can never be deposed. Such a strange, sacred, and inviolable majesty has God imprinted on this faculty; not indeed as upon an absolute, independent sovereign, yet with so great a communication of something next to sovereignty, that while it keeps within its proper compass, it is controllable by no mortal power on earth. For not the greatest monarch in the world can countermand conscience so far as to make it condemn where it would otherwise acquit, or acquit where it would otherwise condemn; no, neither sword nor sceptre can come at it; but it is above and beyond the reach of both."—South. Powerless it may be in the sense that it cannot compel actions according to its decisions. The impress of its authority, however, is so profound and constant, as to amount practically to compulsion or prohibition. And even where action has been committed in defiance of its warning, it haunts the soul with the sense of inevitable judgment. Hamlet finds the way barred which led out of insupportable trouble through the avenue of self-slaughter.

> "Thus conscience does make cowards of us all;
> And thus the native hue of resolution
> Is sicklied o'er with the pale cast of thought;
> And enterprises of great pith and moment,
> With this regard, their currents turn awry,
> And lose the name of action."

mains. Which is to be obeyed, appetite or reflection? Cannot this question be answered from the economy and constitution of human nature merely without saying which is strongest? or need this at all come into consideration? Would not the question be *intelligibly* and fully answered by saying that the principle of reflection or conscience being compared with the various appetites, passions, and affections in men, the former is manifestly superior and chief without regard to strength? And how often soever the latter happens to prevail, it is mere *usurpation*. The former remains in nature and in kind its superior; and every instance of such prevalence of the latter is an instance of breaking in upon, and violation of, the constitution of man.

All this is no more than the distinction which everybody is acquainted with between *mere power* and *authority;* only, instead of being intended to express the difference between what is possible and what is lawful in civil government, here it has been shown applicable to the several principles in the mind of man. Thus, that principle by which we survey, and either approve or disapprove our own heart, temper, and actions, is not only to be considered as what is in its turn to have some in-

---

The murderers of Clarence find it a troublesome impediment in the way of their greed.

"2 *Murd.* Faith, some certain dregs of conscience are yet within me.
1 *Murd.* Remember our reward, when the deed's done.
2 *Murd.* Come, he dies : I had forgot the reward.
1 *Murd.* Where's thy conscience now?
2 *Murd.* In the Duke of Gloster's purse.
1 *Murd.* So, when he opens his purse to give us our reward, thy conscience flies out.
2 *Murd.* 'Tis no matter; let it go : there's few or none will entertain it.
1 *Murd.* What, if it come to thee again?
2 *Murd.* I'll not meddle with it, it is a dangerous thing ; it makes a man a coward ; a man cannot steal, but it accuseth him ; a man cannot swear, but it checks him ; . . . 'Tis a blushing shame-faced spirit, that mutinies in a man's bosom ; it fills one full of obstacles ; it made me once restore a purse of gold that by chance I found ; it beggars any man that keeps it : it is turned out of all towns and cities for a dangerous thing ; and every man that means to live well, endeavours to trust to himself, and live without it."

In short, we have "a thing within us called conscience" (*Titus Andronicus*, Act v. Scene 1), which is "a deity in the bosom" (*Tempest*, Act ii. Scene 1), and, even when disobeyed, overshadows us with the terror of its broken law. The conclusion, therefore, is not merely that conscience has some degree of influence over human nature, but that it is supreme ; and the rebellion of passion, though too often successful, does not diminish this natural superiority.

fluence, which may be said of every passion of the lowest appetites; but likewise as being superior, as from its very nature manifestly claiming superiority over all others, insomuch that you cannot form a notion of this faculty, conscience, without taking in judgment, direction, superintendency. This is a constituent part of the idea, that is, of the faculty itself; and to preside and govern, from the very economy and constitution of man, belongs to it. Had it strength, as it has right; had it power, as it has manifest authority, it would absolutely govern the world.

This gives us a further view of the nature of man; shows us what course of life we were made for, not only that our real nature leads us to be influenced in some degree by reflection and conscience, but likewise in what degree we are to be influenced by it, if we will fall in with and act agreeably to the constitution of our nature; that this faculty was placed within to be our proper governor; to direct and regulate all under principles, passions, and motives of action. This is its right and office; thus sacred is its authority. And how often soever men violate and rebelliously refuse to submit to it for supposed interest which they cannot otherwise obtain, or for the sake of passion which they cannot otherwise gratify, this makes no alteration as to the *natural right* and *office* of conscience.

Let us now turn this whole matter another way,[14] and suppose

---

[14] (4.) Let us now turn this whole matter another way. The conclusion thus positively established is, in the fourth place, set in a clearer light by supposing its opposite to be the truth. Instead of one principle being supreme over the others, all will now be on the same footing, varying only in strength. Now, see to what inferences this would lead. Consider man's actions with respect (1) to himself, (2) to his neighbour, (3) to God. If they are determined by the mere strength of impulse, then (1) and (2) have no limits save these, viz. that no man naturally seeks misery for himself or evil to his neighbour; while (3) has "absolutely no bounds at all." The question, accordingly, is, will any action be congruous with the nature of man, and therefore moral, if it be the product of a sufficiently strong impulse? Will blasphemy be as congruous, and therefore as good and right, as reverence? Will such a deed as parricide be as congruous, and therefore as proper and dutiful, as filial service? The very question reveals the absurdity of the presupposition; and thus we are the more strongly forced back on the position to which we have been led, that conscience has a natural supremacy, and that those actions only are in accordance with human nature of which conscience approves.

there was no such thing at all as this natural supremacy of conscience; that there was no distinction to be made between one inward principle and another, but only that of strength, and see what would be the consequence.

Consider, then, what is the latitude and compass of the actions of man with regard to himself, his fellow-creatures, and the Supreme Being? What are their bounds besides that of natural power? With respect to the first two, they are plainly no other than these: no man seeks misery as such for himself; and no one provoked does mischief to another for its own sake. For in every degree within these bounds, mankind knowingly, from passion or wantonness, bring ruin and misery upon themselves and others; and impiety and profaneness, I mean what every one would call so who believes the being of God, have absolutely no bounds at all. Men blaspheme the Author of nature, formally and in words renounce their allegiance to their Creator. Put an instance, then, with respect to any one of these three. Though we should suppose profane swearing,[15] and in general that kind of impiety now mentioned, to mean nothing, yet it implies wanton disregard and irreverence towards an infinite

---

[15] **Profane swearing.** Man is meant for the fellowship of God; and the deepest utterance of his spiritual being is prayer. The incongruity of this vice with our true nature is practically evinced in this, that it makes prayer an impossibility. "The wise man tells us (Prov. xviii. 10), 'The name of the Lord is a strong tower; the righteous runneth into it, and is safe.' But, alas! what comfort canst thou find in the name of God in thy greatest necessities, since it is the same name thou hast used and worn out before in the meanest and most trivial concerns? Thou hast already talked away the strength and virtue of it, and wilt hardly find more support from it in thy tribulation, than thou gavest reverence unto it in thy conversation" (Hopkins). The same evil effect is seen in a more extended way in the degradation of the whole tone of character, and in the gradually increasing incapacity for and unbelief in things noble and true. "This is what I call debasing the moral currency: lowering the value of every inspiring fact and tradition so that it will command less and less of the spiritual products, the generous motives which sustain the charm and elevation of our social existence—the something besides bread by which man saves his soul alive. . . . Let that moral currency be emptied of its value—let a greedy buffoonery debase all historic beauty, majesty, and pathos, and the more you heap up the desecrated symbols the greater will be the lack of the ennobling emotions which subdue the tyranny of suffering, and make ambition one with social virtue." Theophrastus Such.

Being, our Creator; and is this as suitable to the nature of man as reverence and dutiful submission of heart towards that Almighty Being? Or suppose a man guilty of parricide,[16] with all the circumstances of cruelty which such an action can admit of, this action is done in consequence of its principle being for the present strongest; and if there be no difference between inward principles but only that of strength, the strength being given, you have the whole nature of the man given, so far as it relates to this matter. The action plainly corresponds to the principle, the principle being in that degree of strength it was; it therefore corresponds to the whole nature of the man. Upon comparing the action and the whole nature, there arises no disproportion, there appears no unsuitableness between them. Thus the *murder of a father* and the *nature of man* correspond to each other as the same nature and an act of filial duty. If there be no difference between inward principles, but only that of strength, we can make no distinction between these two actions, considered as the actions of such a creature, but in our coolest hours must approve or disapprove them equally: than which nothing can be reduced to a greater absurdity.

---

[16] **Parricide.** Murders, our Lord says, proceed "out of the heart" (Matt. xv. 19). Paul reckons murders among the "works of the flesh" (Gal. v. 21). That is to say, they have their seat in the impulses and passions of human nature, which, uncontrolled by the authority of a good will, sweep man into the most unnatural and extravagant wickedness. In this sense, that these passions tend to usurp the supremacy of human nature, it is said (1 Tim. i. 9) that the law is not for the righteous, *i.e.* those who are at one with the will expressed in the law, but for "the lawless and disobedient," *i.e.* those who suffer the lower part of their natures to revolt against conscience, among whom are numbered "murderers of fathers and murderers of mothers" as examples of the possible consequences of such revolt.

SERMON III.

THE natural supremacy of reflection or conscience being thus established, we may from it form a distinct notion of what is meant by *human nature*, when virtue is said to consist in following it, and vice in deviating from it. As the idea of a civil constitution [1] implies in it united strength, various subordinations under one direction, that of supreme authority, the different strength of each particular member of the society not coming into the idea; whereas, if you leave out the subordination, the union,

---

[1] **The idea of a civil constitution.** In this paragraph Butler reverts to that conception of human nature which he has established in the preceding sermon. It is not a mere aggregate of appetites, passions, and affections. It is an ordered realm, a civil constitution, or kingdom whose members dwell together under the supremacy of their head, by which their activities are directed and their mutual relations adjusted. That head is conscience. Its authority cannot be defied without the disturbance and threatened dissolution of the commonwealth.

It is interesting to note, as an illustration of the limits of eighteenth century thought, that, while Butler thus treats the individual as a realm or organism, and applies this truth to the practical guidance of life, he does not extend the idea to society as a whole. Yet surely, if man as an individual is a kingdom, the thought which suggests itself immediately is that man in relation to his fellows is member of a kingdom, organ in the wider organism of society. The rule of his life will therefore be that he fulfil this function, and perform the duties of his station, considering others as possessed of similar functions and under the obligation of similar duties. Hence we get the maxim in which Kant summed up moral duty, "to treat others as members of a possible kingdom of ends." It is true indeed that society is not a perfect kingdom, and that we have not done all that is required of us when we have done our duty as good citizens. There is a wider and higher realm, the spiritual sphere which Jesus

and the one direction, you destroy and lose it; so reason, several appetites, passions, and affections, prevailing in different degrees of strength, is not *that* idea or notion of *human nature;* but *that nature* consists in these several principles considered as having a natural respect to each other, in the several passions being naturally subordinate to the one superior principle of reflection or conscience. Every bias, instinct, propension within is a real part of our nature, but not the whole; add to these the superior faculty whose office it is to adjust, manage, and preside over them, and take in this, its natural superiority, and you complete the idea of human nature. And as in civil government the constitution is broken in upon and violated by power and strength prevailing over authority, so the constitutional man is broken in upon and violated by the lower faculties or principles within prevailing over that which is in its nature supreme over them all. Thus, when it is said by ancient writers that tortures and death are not so contrary to human nature as injustice,[2] by this, to be sure, is not meant that the aversion to the former in mankind is less strong and prevalent than their aversion to the latter,

---

called "the Kingdom of God," whose foundations are laid in the Cross. Thus we get three great departments in which the fulfilment of the prayer "Thy kingdom come" is to be realized; the "little kingdom" of the individual man, the wider sphere of society, and highest of all, the kingdom of God. They are closely connected,— the kingdom of God includes them all, — so that the kingdom has not perfectly come in one till God's will is done in the others also. Conscience is the witness in and to the individual of the divine will which is supreme throughout the whole sphere of spiritual being.

[2] **Injustice.** The deep harmony between justice and human nature, even amid the presence of pain and misery; the utter incongruity between injustice and human nature, amid whatever circumstances of external happiness or prosperity, may be illustrated from a well-known passage in Plato's *Republic*. Two pictures are presented, the just man who is deemed unjust, the unjust man who has the reputation of justice. The former "will be scourged, racked, bound, will have his eyes burnt out, and at last, after suffering every kind of evil, he will be impaled." The latter "bears rule in the city; he can marry whom he will, and give in marriage to whom he will; also he can trade and deal where he likes, and always to his own advantage, because he has no misgivings as to injustice;" and possesses numerous other similar advantages (*Republic*, Book ii., Jowett's translation). It needs no proof which of these is true to human nature, or in whom is realized the soul's true harmony.

but that the former is only contrary to our nature, considered in a partial view, and which takes in only the lowest part of it, that which we have in common with the brutes, whereas the latter is contrary to our nature, considered in a higher sense, as a system and constitution, contrary to the whole economy of man (*a*).

(*a*) Every man in his physical nature is one individual single agent. He has likewise properties and principles, each of which may be considered separately and without regard to the respects which they have to each other. Neither of these are the nature we are taking a view of. But it is the inward frame of man, considered as a *system or constitution*, whose several parts are united, not by a physical principle of individuation, but by the respects they have to each other; the chief of which is the subjection which the appetites, passions, and particular affections have to the one supreme principle of reflection or conscience. The system or constitution is formed by, and consists in, these respects and this subjection. Thus the body is a *system or constitution;* so is a tree, so is every machine.[3] Consider all the

---

[3] The body . . . a tree, a machine. These are each an illustration of what is meant by a *system* or *constitution*, and aid in completing our notion of human nature as itself such a constitution. We might place them in an ascending scale ; *a machine* in which the parts are adjusted by application of external force and skill ; *a tree*, which is a unity in so far as with its branches, etc., it makes one living whole, but which exhibits little variety or complexity of structure ; *a body*, in which this variety and complexity reaches a high pitch of development, while all the various parts are yet held within the unity of the organism ; *human nature*, in which we have a subtlety of distinction and elaboration of parts unknown in the physical world, and, at the same time, a unity likewise in these lower stages unknown, the unity of self-conscious personality or of conscience. So far the analogy is helpful. But when Butler proceeds to infer that "some degree of disorder" must be looked for in such a creature as man, the use of the figure is questionable. A superiority maintained in a position of unstable equilibrium, threatened with continual deposition, would be a very imperfect basis of morality, and would be apt to produce a scepticism of good that might easily prove productive of tolerance of evil. To be good, we must have a guarantee that good *is;* and in doing good, we must know ourselves the instruments of a good already perfected. To a good which is already victorious, and has been wrought out for us, conscience testifies. Thus the commands which it imposes upon us are at the same time prophecies of their perfect fulfilment by us, and all our tasks, as we yield to the will of God, are

And from all these things put together, nothing can be more evident than that, exclusive of revelation, man cannot be considered as a creature left by his Maker to act at random, and live at large up to the extent of his natural power, as passion, humour, wilfulness happen to carry him, which is the condition brute creatures are in; but that, *from his make, constitution, or nature, he is, in the strictest and most proper sense, a law to himself.* He hath the rule of right within;[4] what is wanting is only that he honestly attend to it.

---

several parts of a tree, without the natural respects they have to each other, and you have not at all the idea of a tree; but add these respects and this gives you the idea. The body may be impaired by sickness, a tree may decay, a machine be out of order, and yet the system and constitution of them not totally dissolved. There is plainly somewhat which answers to all this in the moral constitution of man. Whoever will consider his own nature will see that the several appetites, passions, and particular affections have different respects among themselves. They are restraints upon, and are in proportion to each other. This proportion is just and perfect when all those under principles are perfectly coincident with conscience, so far as their nature permits, and in all cases under its absolute and entire direction. The least excess or defect, the least alteration of the due proportions amongst themselves, or of their coincidence with conscience, though not proceeding into action, is some degree of disorder in the moral constitution. But perfection, though plainly intelligible and supposable, was never attained by any man. If the higher principle of reflection maintains its place, and, as much as it can, corrects that disorder, and hinders it from breaking out into action, that is all that can be expected in such a creature as man. And though the appetites and passions have not their exact due proportion to each other, though they often strive for mastery with judgment or reflection; yet, since the superiority of this principle to all others is the chief respect which forms the constitution, so far as this superiority is maintained, the character, the man, is good, worthy, virtuous.

---

performed with an infinite energy of good which is destined to obtain complete fulfilment.

[4] **The rule of right within.** In considering the statement which Butler here makes, we must remember his theory of the nature of conscience, whose inadequacy and inconsistency with other and higher ideas to be found in his writings we have endeavoured to point out in the Introduction. He regards conscience as a faculty to be found in man, about which you can say no more than just that it is there. This faculty provides "the rule of right," and men will do

right, and be moral and virtuous, if they obey the dictates of this
faculty. He was able, therefore, to regard conscience as an independent authority, competent in its own right to produce virtuous
characters. He could, accordingly, appeal to those who rejected
revelation, and offer to them conscience as of itself sufficient to lead
them into virtue. He says in effect, "You will admit surely that
virtue is the best course of life. Revelation prescribes it; but
unhappily you do not believe in revelation. Conscience, quite in-
dependently of religion, prescribes the same thing. Attend honestly
to what conscience says, and you will attain virtue." We have seen,
however, being taught in part by Butler himself, that this view of
conscience, and of the consequent relation of morality and religion, is
inadequate and misleading. Conscience is not an independent and
self-sufficient faculty, and morality is not an alternative to religion as
a means of producing virtue. Conscience is the faculty, if we like to
put it so, by which we apprehend what is good or right when presented to us as a possible end of action ; and this, when we pursue
it with deliberate intent, secures the satisfaction and harmony of our
being. Or, what is the same thing from the other side, it is the good
witnessing for itself in a nature which was meant for its pursuit.
The highest good for man is the will or purpose of God. Conscience,
therefore, testifies to man regarding the purpose in fulfilling which
man is realizing his true self. "The rule of right" is not "within,"
but without in the will of God. What is right is not determined by
the *ipse dixit* of an independent faculty which when interrogated will
always give the same oracular responses in all ages and under all
conditions. We learn what we *ought to do*, just as we learn other
facts, from observation of the various forms in which God reveals His
mind to us. Conscience descends from its proud position as an
infallible teacher, and becomes itself a humble learner in the school of
a divine education. In the education of conscience we may note
three stages or classes, so to speak. (1) The institutions of society,
the sacred rights of life, honour, property, repute, with all the detailed
obligations to which these give rise. We cannot slip this class and
pass at once to some higher department. Admitting and maintaining that morality is not sufficient to itself, we must remember that
our higher aims and aspirations will not be justified unless we have
"travelled the common highway of reason — the life of the good
neighbour and honest citizen;" and we "can never forget" that we are
"still only on a further stage of the same journey" (Green's *Introduction to Hume*, vol. ii. p. 71). To neglect these things is to obscure
the testimony of conscience, and to make it dumb in the great moral
crises of life. (2) The record of God's special dealings with man
contained in the Bible. Apart from any particular theory of inspira-

should denominate our actions good or evil, are in many respects of great service. Yet let any plain, honest man, before he engages in any course of action, ask himself, Is this I am going about right, or is it wrong?[5] Is it good, or is it evil? I

---

tion, it will be generally admitted that the history of Israel and the life of Christ constitute the highest expression of God's purpose for man. Conscience, therefore, we may boldly say, will be inarticulate or misleading, save as we read ourselves into the heart of the Bible, and conform to the "rule of right" therein contained. (3) The immediate dealing of God's Spirit with the human soul. Of the forms and occasions of such tuition it is impossible to speak in general terms. No human being lives who has not been thus divinely tutored. At such times conscience, the "soul's large window," is lifted high, and we gaze with open eye into the will of God. In these ways then is conscience educated, and thus informed testifies to us of that good and right which in these ways is revealed. "The rule of right," to the apprehension of which we are thus brought, is no imposition from an alien sphere. It is the revelation of what in ideal truth we are. When apprehended in loyal obedience, it becomes the energy by which we reach this the goal of our being. For we are not under law, but under grace.

[5] **Is this I am going about right, or is it wrong?** Do there really arise circumstances in which this question could not be answered? Do we ever find ourselves inextricably fixed on the horns of a moral dilemma? Can there be such a thing as a conscience which finds itself unable to give a direct and satisfactory decision? In considering the subject of perplexity of conscience, we must be careful to distinguish cases of apparent from those of real perplexity. (1) There is one case which Butler has here noted, and which needs only to be stated to be exposed, viz. "partiality to ourselves." Here the verdict of conscience is in itself quite clear and distinct, but is opposed by strong passion or imperious self-interest, which clamorously demands to be obeyed. This is obviously no genuine perplexity *of conscience.* The perplexity is caused by the evil impulse. The worst thing to do in such a case is to discuss it. This means no more than dallying with sin and ultimately yielding to it. What an evil conscience will thus do in an individual case, casuistry seeks to reduce to a system of universal applicability. Casuistry holds the rule of right to be embodied in a code containing an elaborate series of regulations. The sole question which it asks with respect to any possible action is, Can it be reduced under one or other of these regulations? Suppose, then, a man wants very much to do something which is forbidden, or to evade something which is prescribed, in some one of these rules, the ingenuity of the casuist is devoted to finding some peculiarity in the circumstances which will permit the act to be referred to some other rule, according to which permission is granted

to do it or not to do it, as the case may be. The famous *Provincial Letters* of Pascal are full of instances of casuistical reasoning by which lying, thieving, killing, etc., are under certain circumstances pronounced lawful. (2) Sometimes cases occur in which the clear testimony of conscience is confronted with some instinct of the soul, itself true and noble. Such a case is that of Jeanie Deans, in the *Heart of Midlothian.* Conscience imposes on her the duty of unswerving truthfulness. Love to her sister pleads that she ought to tell one slight falsehood and so save her sister's life. Here there is genuine perplexity, though still not *of conscience.* Conscience speaks calmly and clearly. In such a case we have to note such points as these :—1. We are in duty bound to take all possible pains to satisfy the demand of conscience. We must take care that our perplexity is not really reluctance to undergo the pains of vindicating the right, a desire to escape trouble by soaring away on wings of sentiment, instead of climbing the steep path of duty. Jeanie was too honest to justify falsehood by giving it a fine name. She could not tell a lie, but she could walk barefoot to London to save her sister. 2. We are to consider whether, in holding to the testimony of conscience, even at the expense of dire consequences to those whom our instinct teaches us to rescue from all pains and penalties, we are not in truth seeking their highest welfare. Would it not be better for them to endure the suffering rather than miss the discipline? We are to think, too, not of individuals but of humanity, for whose sake we are bound to preserve inviolate the conditions of worthy living. The rigour of Angelo, though falsified by his after conduct, makes noble justification of itself when Isabella pleads with him to show mercy :

> "I show it most of all, when I show justice;
> For then I pity those I do not know,
> Which a dismissed offence would after gall;
> And do him right, that, answering one foul wrong,
> Lives not to act another."
> *Measure for Measure,* Act ii. Scene 2

(3) "Perplexity of conscience, properly so called, seems always to arise from conflict between different formulæ for expressing the ideal of good in human conduct, or between different institutions for furthering its realization, which have alike obtained authority over men's minds without being intrinsically entitled to more than a partial and relative obedience; or from the incompatibility of some such formula or institution on the one side, with some moral impulse of the individual on the other, which is really an impulse towards the attainment of human perfection, but cannot adjust itself to recognised rules and established institutions" (Green's *Prolegomena*, p. 342. The whole chapter is a masterly exposition of the function of conscience, and contains the soundest and loftiest ethical teaching).

answered agreeably to truth and virtue by almost any fair man in almost any circumstance. Neither do there appear any cases which

---

A man may be perplexed as to whether he is to obey the Church or the State when their commands conflict, both of which claim an absolute, though entitled only to a relative, obedience. Or he may be perplexed as to whether he is to obey either Church or State when against one or other of them his convictions of right rise in revolt. In all this there is no conflict of duty. Duty under all circumstances is always one. He is perplexed to know what his duty is. Whence shall light arise upon his darkness? No categorical answer is possible. Life would lose its moral significance if there were some oracle which could take the task of decision in such cases out of our hands altogether. We are prepared for such crises by faithfulness to plain duty maintained habitually. Obedience is the organ of moral no less than of spiritual enlightenment. "The only safeguard of virtue is the healthy prompting of a nature accustomed to act rightly, and sincerely desirous of doing so" (Mackintosh, *Christ and the Jewish Law*, p. 48. The whole chapter, entitled "Christ's criticism of the Pharisees," is helpful in studying the effects of all external systems of ethics). To the question, "How am I to know what is right? the answer must be, By the $\alpha\ddot{\iota}\sigma\theta\eta\sigma\iota\varsigma$ of the $\varphi\rho\acute{o}\nu\iota\mu o\varsigma$" (Bradley's *Ethical Studies*, p. 177); and the $\varphi\rho\acute{o}\nu\iota\mu o\varsigma$ is the man who has learned God's will by habitually doing it. The man who is thus educated by obedience has reached a standpoint from which he can estimate the value of the authorities that claim his submission. He can distinguish between them when they compete, as the Roman Catholics of England did in the great Armada conflict, when they fought for the Queen against the Pope. He can even transgress them in name of a higher authority, whose voice he has heard behind him saying, This is the way, as when those oppressed have risen against their oppressors. The highest vindication of such rebellion against authority is when the principle which inspired the revolt becomes the authority of the generation following. Thus the ideal of truth grows from age to age, the authority, which was for a time its expression, becoming its tyrant, till those who know and love the truth set it free to express itself in higher and fuller forms.

There is no such thing, therefore, as an ultimate perplexity of conscience. Conscience will always testify to the highest good. But if we are to hear its deliverances aright, and not to mingle with them the importunities of desire or the impetuosities of self-will, we must have learned always to prefer the good, and in the manifold details of life to do the will of God. It is on such presupposition of habitual obedience that we can trust our heart, and say with the hero whom Wordsworth has idealized,—

"*That* tells me what to do."
Rob Roy's Grave.

look like exceptions to this, but those of superstition and of partiality to ourselves. Superstition may, perhaps, be somewhat of an exception; but partiality to ourselves is not; this being itself dishonesty. For a man to judge that to be the equitable, the moderate, right part for him to act, which he would see to be hard, unjust, oppressive in another; this is plain vice, and can proceed only from great unfairness of mind. But, allowing that mankind hath the rule of right within himself, yet it may be asked, "What obligations are we under[6] to attend and follow it?" I answer: it has been proved, that man by his nature is a law to himself, without the particular distinct consideration of the positive sanctions of that law; the rewards and punishments[7] which we

---

[6] **What obligations are we under?** The mere statement of this question makes us feel instinctively that it ought not to be put. Morality we feel is an end in itself. It must be pursued for its own sake. If we performed an action, in itself good, for the sake of some result which was not in itself good, we could claim no credit for the doing of it. It would not be, so far as we are concerned, a virtuous action. But underlying the question, "Why must I do what is right?" there is the unexpressed theory that we can be induced or compelled to do what is right only on grounds that lie outside the consideration of what is right; or, what comes to the same thing, that morality has a claim upon us only as a means to some end beyond itself. And this our moral sense resents as a degradation of morality. The man who should ask, "What good shall I get, or what evil shall I escape, by being moral?" we should see had not reached a truly moral standpoint, even if we did not already suspect him of being immoral. The only question we can legitimately put is, "What is the end proposed in morality?" And this is the question of the first efforts of the human spirit as it seeks a practical solution to the problem of life. The question is, "What is the chief end of man?" That determined, there is no further question of "Why?"

[7] **Rewards and punishments.** Butler here denies that the motives for observing the rule of right are the rewards and punishments annexed to it. The theory which asserts what Butler here denies is to be found in the moral system of Paley (1743-1805). Virtue, according to his well-known definition, is "the doing good to mankind, in obedience to the will of God, and for the sake of everlasting happiness." The law or rule of right, accordingly, is the will of God, and the motive for obedience to it is derived from consideration of the rewards and punishments which are annexed to it, and which are bestowed in a future state. He asks precisely the question which we have just seen ought not to be put, and in a particular instance discusses the question, "Why am I obliged to keep my word?" The answer to which is, in accordance with his conception of virtue,

feel, and those which, from the light of reason, we have ground to believe are annexed to it. The question, then, carries its own answer along with it. Your obligation to obey [8] this law, is its

---

"The pains and penalties which would be inflicted on me if I broke it, the reward held out to me if I kept it." This brutally plain appeal to the lowest and most selfish motives strikes us at once as most repulsive and utterly false to the character of God and the facts of human nature. Besides, if pressed as the sole reason why we should be moral, it leaves the whole basis of morality in a most precarious state. Suppose a man—and he would not be an ignoble man either, such an one as the Gothic chief who refused Christian baptism when he heard his heathen ancestors were in hell, saying he would not be separated from the heroes of his race—were to defy the whole scheme of reward and punishment, and say, "I care nothing for your heaven, and I will risk your hell rather than do the things required in your law;" what more have you to say to him, what further appeal to urge? You have played your last card, and he walks away the victor. Of course this is no proof that there are not rewards and punishments in a future state. But it is sufficient proof that they cannot be made the sole motives for righteousness. Rewards and punishments are indeed the illustration in the sphere of after event of what right and wrong in themselves inherently *are*. Penalty is not arbitrarily attached to sin, but is its inevitable recoil upon the sinner's head. It cannot therefore be used as a mere threat, "Take care, or—;" it can only be used as an exhibition to the sinner of what his sin is; *i.e.* penalty must always be conceived in reference to the moral consciousness of man, and never in relation to his mere selfish instinct for avoiding unpleasant consequences. Terror is, indeed, used in Scripture as an argument, but it is the terror *of the Lord*, the dread of trespassing the law of eternal right, not the coward fear of torment. The whole passage in which the phrase occurs is as far removed as possible from appeal to baser feelings, and is thoroughly ethical: "Knowing therefore the terror of the Lord, we persuade men; but we are made manifest unto God; and I trust also are made manifest in your consciences" (2 Cor. v. 11). The same passage has also higher motives still: "The love of Christ constraineth us" (ver. 14); and "if any man be in Christ, he is a new creature" (ver. 17). The terror of violated right, the love of the redeemed, the ambition of the renewed will, determined on achieving God's own ideal for man, form an ascending scale of motive leading towards holy living.

[8] **Your obligation to obey.** Whence then comes the obligation to obey, if not from the rewards and punishments annexed to the rule of right? Butler answers, from the rule itself. It carries its obligation with it. Authenticated as it is by the facts of human nature, it comes to us with an authority which is ultimate and unquestionable. It

being the law of your nature. That your conscience approves of
and attests to such a course of action, is itself alone an obligation. Conscience does not only offer itself to show us the way
we should walk in, but it likewise carries its own authority with
it, that it is our natural guide, the guide assigned us by the

---

remains for us to follow the path of duty thus indicated, steep and
rough though it be, with no sidelong glances at some by-way which
might conduct to ends of pleasure without seeming to deviate to a
dangerous extent from the straight line of right. Such language as
Butler here uses rings true, and stands in noble contrast to the
constant quest for motive which characterizes a different school of
ethical teachers. Every loyal heart responds to the sentiment that
we must do our duty for duty's sake, asking no question about self-
interest. It is possible, however, so to state this principle as to
involve ourselves in a onesidedness the opposite of that criticised in
the preceding note ; and perhaps a lurking sense of this led Butler
to his vindication of the identity of virtue and self-interest which
occupies the concluding sections of this Sermon, and which jars on
us after the purity and loftiness of his last utterances. On the one
side is the theory mentioned above, which traces all ethical motive to
individual pleasure and pain. On the other is the theory of Butler,
which is very much that of Kant in a later day, which declares that
action alone to be good which is done under the sheer sense of a categorical imperative, "Thou shalt," "Thou shalt not." Rigorously carried
out, this would end in a gloomy asceticism, whose sole attitude towards
the right is that of awe and dread, and which seeks to expel from
the motives of action all taint of delight, and to reduce them to the
one principle of fear. Hence, as has been pointed out, follows the
ridiculous consequence that, properly speaking, we can never be said
to do right, except when we do it reluctantly and against our will.
We rise above both these abstract theories, when we ask what is the
right whose command, intimated to us by conscience, we are bound
to obey? The answer to which Butler himself, in the Sermons to
which reference has been made in the Introduction, conducts us, is
that good will or love of God which has created the sphere in which
we achieve the ideal of our nature, with its ever widening circles of
interest, the family, civil society, the state, and whatever wider
domain of action is open to man. This, then, comes to us with the
stern imperative of law only when it remains above, beyond, or
against us, something with which we are not yet thoroughly at one.
When, however, we do surrender to it heart and soul, it is no longer
an external force operative against our will ; it is an inner impulse
with which our wills are one, whose operation is the joy of our whole
being. The Cross of Christ, when taken up in the same spirit of self-
denial in which He bore it to Calvary, becomes for us, through His
grace, a yoke that is easy, a burden that is light.

author of our nature. It therefore belongs to our condition of being : it is our duty to walk in that path, and follow this guide, without looking about to see whether we may not possibly forsake them with impunity. However, let us hear what is to be said against obeying this law of our nature. And the sum is no more than this : "Why should we be concerned [9] about anything out of and beyond ourselves? If we do find within ourselves regards to others, and restraints of we know not how many different kinds; yet these being embarrassments, and hindering us from going the nearest way to our own good, why should we not endeavour to suppress and get over them?"

Thus people go on with words, which, when applied to human nature, and the condition in which it is placed in this world, have really no meaning. For does not all this kind of talk go upon supposition that our happiness in this world consists in somewhat quite distinct from regards to others, and that it is the privilege of vice to be without restraint [10] or confinement?

---

[9] **Why should we be concerned.** It is just possible, as has been remarked above, that Butler feared lest his claim for virtue might seem too high, abstract, and superhuman. Certainly it was a claim which the votaries of pleasure would be little likely to acknowledge. He may therefore have thought it incumbent upon him, as a moral teacher, not to alienate if possible even the pleasure-seekers. He endeavours accordingly, in these closing sections, to show that, after all, virtue carries off the palm from all competitors as a mean toward pleasure. It is, to say the least, a very precarious attempt, as much so in success as in failure. Far better to allow virtue to defend itself, and to leave the discovery of the satisfaction which it affords to those who are willing to sacrifice all to this service, without pausing to reflect that they will lose little or nothing by their decision. In the words of a modern essayist, "We shall do well, I think, to avoid all praises of the pleasantness of virtue. We may believe that it transcends all possible delights of vice, but it would be well to remember that we desert a moral point of view, that we degrade and prostitute virtue, when to those who do not love her for herself, we bring ourselves to recommend her for the sake of her pleasures. Against the base mechanical βαναυσία, which meets us on all sides, with its 'what is the use' of goodness, beauty, or truth, there is but one fitting answer from the friends of science, or art, or religion and virtue, 'We do not know, and we do not care'" (*Bradley's Ethical Studies*, p. 57).

[10] **Privilege of vice to be without restraint.** In the first place, accordingly, Butler supposes the friends of pleasure to ask, "Why should we submit to the restraints of virtue? Why should we not seek what we wish untrammelled by any restrictions?" To this

Whereas, on the contrary, the enjoyments, in a manner all the

---

Butler answers in effect, "If the question be of restraint, there is as much restraint in vice as in virtue. The truth is, absolute freedom from restraint is for us impossible, constituted as we are. Whatever end we seek, even though it be a purely selfish one, we must submit to the restraint of certain means. And it frequently happens that unrestrained gratification of desire so obviously entails direful consequences, that even a wicked man will decline to pay such price for liberty." Thus to defend virtue by the argument that it involves no more restraint than vice, is, however, too low ground to take. A truer answer might have been found by further consideration of what freedom really means, and by properly distinguishing between liberty and licence. If freedom means negation of restraint, then freedom never was. Strip a man of all restraint, and what you have left is something about which you can make no moral affirmation. It is neither good nor bad, because moral action is impossible to it. Infamy and honour, as Butler well observes, ambition, covetousness, the disgrace of poverty, the reputation of riches, would, the one as little as the other, evoke response; for it would be deaf and blind to the moral world in which men live and move and have their being. The attempt to be free in this sense, therefore, would amount to an endeavour after spiritual suicide. A man is what he is through the relations in which he is situated, as father, brother, friend, etc. He attains the ideal of his being, the determined purpose of God for him, when, surrendering his private will, he lives in and for these relationships; and then and then only is he free. As long as he resents them and withholds from them his service, they are limits and restraints of the most irksome kind. When, however, he accepts them and makes his own the divine purpose expressed in them, they become the conditions at once of his highest attainment and of his freedom. Licence, therefore, when it breaks these bonds, and sets forth in the career of self-will, is so far from being the freedom whose name it vauntingly bears, that it is already inherently the opposite of freedom, the bondage of the spirit, the effectual barrier in the way of all true attainment; and this it will soon exhibit in the sphere of outward event, and will even in the eyes of the world terminate in the bondage it claimed to have destroyed. The highest answer to Butler's supposed antagonists is that true freedom is to be found in the pursuit of virtue alone.

"*Lucio.* Why, how now, Claudio? whence comes this restraint?
Claudio. From too much liberty, my Lucio, liberty;
As surfeit is the father of much fast,
So every scope by the immoderate use
Turns to restraint: Our natures do pursue
(Like rats that ravin down their proper bane)
A thirsty evil, and when we drink we die."
Measure for Measure, Act i. Scene 3.

common enjoyments of life, even the pleasures of vice, depend upon these regards of one kind or another to our fellow-creatures. Throw off all regards to others, and we should be quite indifferent to infamy and to honour: there could be no such thing at all as ambition, and scarce any such thing as covetousness; for we should likewise be equally indifferent to the disgrace of poverty, the several neglects and kinds of contempt which accompany this state, and to the reputation of riches, the regard and respect they usually procure. Neither is restraint by any means peculiar to one course of life; but our very nature, exclusive of conscience, and our condition, lays us under an absolute necessity of it. We cannot gain any end whatever without being confined to the proper means, which is often the most painful and uneasy confinement. And, in numberless instances, a present appetite cannot be gratified without such apparent and immediate ruin and misery, that the most dissolute man in the world chooses to forego the pleasure than endure the pain.

Is the meaning, then, to indulge those regards to our fellow-creatures, and submit to those restraints which, upon the whole, are attended with more satisfaction than uneasiness, and get over only those which bring more uneasiness and inconvenience than satisfaction? "Doubtless this was our meaning."[11] You have

---

[11] *Doubtless this was our meaning.* Butler now, in the second place, supposes his antagonist to contend that he did not mean to cast off all restraint, but simply to choose such course of action as should be attended with the least inconvenience and the greatest satisfaction. "Precisely," says Butler, "that is what I wish you to do; and the course of action which yields the greatest satisfaction is virtue." It has already been pointed out, that to make the advantages attendant on virtue the chief argument for its pursuit, is a very precarious vindication of its claims. As a statement of fact, however, Butler's remarks in this section are unexceptionable. It is quite true that rage, envy, and restraint are productive of misery; compassion and benevolence of a very pure delight; that riches and power yield no such satisfaction as justice, honesty, charity; that virtue and a good mind spread a peace through the soul unknown to the ambitious and the covetous. It is most certain that vice is a hard taskmaster, under whose thraldom many a sinner is groaning, hating the fetters he has fastened on his soul; while virtue, especially when it has become that habit which is a second, and, in this case, our true nature, is the very ease and energy of our being. These are aspects of the subject upon which it is impossible to lay too much emphasis; provided always it be

changed sides, then.—Keep to this: be consistent with yourselves, and you and the men of virtue are, in general, perfectly agreed. But let us take care, and avoid mistakes. Let it not be taken for granted that the temper of envy, rage, resentment, yields greater delight than meekness, forgiveness, compassion, and goodwill: especially when it is acknowledged that rage, envy, resentment, are in themselves mere misery; and the satisfaction arising from the indulgence of them is little more than relief from that misery; whereas the temper of compassion and benevolence is itself delightful; and the indulgence of it, by doing good, affords new positive delight and enjoyment. Let it not be taken for granted that the satisfaction arising from the reputation of riches and power, however obtained, and from the respect paid to them, is greater than the satisfaction arising from the reputation of justice, honesty, charity, and the esteem which is universally acknowledged to be their due. And if it be doubtful which of these satisfactions is the greatest, as there are persons who think neither of them very considerable, yet there can be no doubt concerning ambition and covetousness, virtue, and a good mind, considered in themselves, and as leading to different courses of life; there can, I say, be no doubt which temper and which course is attended with most peace and tranquillity of mind, which with most perplexity, vexation, and inconvenience. And both the virtues and vices which have been now mentioned, do in a manner equally imply in them regards of one kind or another to our fellow-creatures. And with respect to restraint and confinement, whoever will

---

understood we are not thereby endeavouring to recommend virtue to those who do not love her, as children are coaxed to swallow medicine by promise of abundant sweets. We may admit that even in the world duty seldom clashes with interest, honesty being, if we are to believe what we are told, the best policy. We most distinctly hold that, in the highest sense, duty and interest, man's best interest, are one. The use of this truth, however, is not to bribe the immoral to abandon their evil ways. Their case is not simply that of those who have made a mistake. Vice is more than a blunder; it is a crime. To those who gaze upon her with reluctance, virtue wears the stern aspect of law, and offers nothing as consolation for abandonment of vice. To those who fall at her feet in reverence, she reveals herself in gracious guise of Love, and bestows her treasures of peace and joy freely upon those who, expecting nothing in return, give up all for her. "Seek *first* the Kingdom of God and His righteousness, and all these things shall be added unto you."

consider the restraints from fear and shame, the dissimulation, mean arts of concealment, servile compliances, one or other of which belong to almost every course of vice, will soon be convinced that the man of virtue is by no means upon a disadvantage in this respect. How many instances are there in which men feel, and own, and cry aloud under the chains of vice with which they are enthralled, and which yet they will not shake off! How many instances in which persons manifestly go through more pain and self-denial to gratify a vicious passion than would have been necessary to the conquest of it! To this is to be added that when virtue is become habitual, when the temper of it is acquired, what was before confinement ceases to be so by becoming choice and delight. Whatever restraint and guard upon ourselves may be needful to unlearn any unnatural distortion or odd gesture, yet in all propriety of speech, natural behaviour must be the most easy and unrestrained. It is manifest that in the common course of life there is seldom any inconsistency between our duty and what is called interest; it is much seldomer that there is an inconsistency between duty and what is really our present interest, meaning by interest, happiness and satisfaction. Self-love, then, though confined to the interests of the present world, does in general perfectly coincide with virtue, and leads us to one and the same course of life. But, whatever exceptions there are to this, which are much fewer than they are commonly thought, all shall be set right [12] at the final distri-

---

[12] **All shall be set right.** The connection between a virtuous life and "the hope of glory" is one which lies on the borderland between morality and religion. All ethical teachers who have dealt profoundly with their subject, have felt that its issues led into another world than that of space and time, and have endeavoured in various ways to trace the connecting lines between the two. Plato found that the mighty distinctions of good and evil, justice and injustice, are not sufficiently emphasized in any finite experiences; and thus in the closing sections of the Republic seeks to find more adequate expression for them in the judgment of another world. The Myth or Vision of Er touches the highest point of Greek speculation, and in beauty of form and depth of thought is worthy to be placed beside the dream of him who followed Virgil through the shades. It ends in these memorable words: "Wherefore my counsel is, that we hold fast to the heavenly way, and follow after justice and virtue always, considering that the soul is immortal, and able to endure every sort of good and every sort of evil. Thus shall we live, dear to one another and to the gods, both while remaining here, and when,

bution of things. It is a manifest absurdity to suppose evil prevailing finally over good under the conduct and administration of a perfect mind.

---

like conquerors in the games who go round to gather gifts, we receive our reward. And it shall be well with us both in this life and in the pilgrimage of a thousand years which we have been reciting." The idea which the Greek found necessary to complete his system, could scarcely be absent from theories that have felt the influence of Christianity. Two forms of the connection between immortality and virtue may be noticed : (1) That of Butler, in this place ; according to which immortality is required to allow of the good man attaining perfect happiness ; and (2) That of Kant, according to which immortality is required to allow of the man who wishes to be good attaining perfect goodness. Neither theory can be regarded as satisfactory. On Butler's theory, the happiness of a future state is one of the incidental advantages of virtue. Even if interest should not in this life be evidently on the side of virtue, this will be evident afterwards, and the virtuous man will find himself in the position of a successful speculator who has held on to his stock while others were selling off, and now after a sudden and unexpected " rise " awakes a millionaire, while they are bankrupt. But thus to present virtue as a prosperous investment is to degrade its purity, and is beneath the level of Butler's plainest teaching. Kant's theory is more profound, and is at least not liable to this objection. The difficulty here lies as to the nature of morality and the conditions of moral experience. If it were possible for the individual confronted with the imperative of duty ever fully to comply with its demands, and thus by unaided effort to attain the goal of perfect righteousness ; then, in the case of persons of sufficient strength of purpose, it would be enough to give them ample time in order that they might reach the end of their endeavour; and Kant's doctrine of immortality would stand. If, however, this is not the case,—if from the point of view of mere morality the moral life is an endless conflict between the command of law and the revolt of passion,—if the goal of achieved goodness be by the very statement of the terms of its pursuit an impossibility,— then the matter is not mended by the most liberal allowance of time ; and even endless time would be insufficient for the purpose. We are therefore forced back to the question which, both in the Introduction and in these Notes, has forced itself in various forms upon us, viz. How is morality possible? What is the true basis of Ethics ? The answer, to which we have been conducted as it seems to us inevitably by every pathway of reflection, is that morality grounds itself on religion, which offers to us at the beginning what mere morality faintly hopes for in the end, and that we can hope to live the moral life only from the standpoint of a union, already effected through surrender, between us and the will which is to be done in earth as in

The whole argument which I have been now insisting upon, may be thus summed up and given you in one view. The nature of man is adapted to some course of action or other. Upon comparing some actions with this nature, they appear suitable and correspondent to it; from comparison of other actions with the same nature, there arises to our view some unsuitableness or disproportion. The correspondence of actions

---

heaven. A new view of the connection between immortality and virtue now emerges. The connection is seen to be twofold. (1) It appears at the starting-point of the moral life. That starting-point is reconciliation, the union of our individual finite being with the infinite and eternal being of God. When, dying to self, we rise in Christ into newness of life, the life which we now possess is already eternal, for He *is* the resurrection and the life. We can be virtuous, therefore, only because ours in Christ is an eternal life. The notion of time prolonged into endlessness disappears. Quantity gives way to quality. We hope to achieve goodness because there works within us the energy of a goodness that is infinite and unfailing. We may say with Kant that we need eternity to make us good; but it is an eternity that is present and not merely the possibility of a hereafter. (2) It appears at the goal of the experience which is limited to space and time. We are under a discipline of incompleteness. As we lift the broken threads of our life, we cry in great yearning for a time when even these shall be woven into harmony. The literature of the world is full of this cry, which is indeed but the earnest expectation of the creature waiting for the manifestation of the sons of God. This, which is the inarticulate prophecy of all pain and sorrow, is the revelation of God in Christ. The completeness longed for *is* in God's eternally finished purpose, and therefore *shall be* even in the experience of these throbbing hearts. How perfect shall be the attainment, how full and detailed the explanation, who shall say? Browning, mourning over a fair life cut short, can say,

> "But the time will come,—at last it will,
>   When, Evelyn Hope, what meant (I shall say)
> In the lower earth, in the years long still,
>   That body and soul so pure and gay?
> Why your hair was amber, I shall divine,
>   And your mouth of your own geranium's red,
> And what you would do with me, in fine,
>   In the new life come in the old one's stead."

And not only physical beauty thus early blighted, but plans nobly formed, tasks taken up in heroic self-denial, characters opening in divine proportions, all things fair and good, which here have been left broken and incomplete, shall then receive their interpretation and fulfilment. Priceless is such "sure and certain hope." It stimulates

to the nature of the agent renders them natural; their disproportion to it, unnatural. That an action is correspondent to the nature of the agent, does not arise from its being agreeable to the principle which happens to be the strongest; for it may be so, and yet be quite disproportionate to the nature of the agent. The correspondence, therefore, or disproportion, arises from somewhat else. This can be nothing but a difference in nature and kind (altogether distinct from strength) between the inward principles. Some, then, are in nature and kind superior to others. And the correspondence arises from the action being conformable to the higher principle, and the unsuitableness from its being contrary to it. Reasonable self-love and conscience are the chief or superior principles in the nature of man, because an action may be suitable to this nature, though all other principles be violated, but becomes unsuitable if either of those are. Conscience and self-love, if we understand our true happiness, always lead us the same way.—Duty and interest are perfectly coincident; for the most part in this world, but entirely, and in every instance, if we take in the future, and the whole; this being implied in the notion of a good and perfect administration of things. Thus, they who have been so wise in their generation as to regard only their own supposed interest at the expense and to the injury of others, shall at last find that he who has given up all the advantages of the present world rather than violate his conscience and the relations of life, has infinitely better provided for himself, and secured his own interest and happiness.

---

our energies that flag under strain of unrewarded toil and depression of continued disappointment. We feel that we can, and

> "Must still believe, for still we hope
> That, in a world of larger scope,
> What here is faithfully begun
> Will be completed, not undone."

It shines above us as the morning star, amid deepest consciousness of personal shortcoming and unworthiness. "It doth not yet appear what we shall be; but we know that when He shall appear we shall be like Him, for we shall see Him as he is. And every man that hath this hope in him purifieth himself, even as He is pure."

THE END.

www.ingramcontent.com/pod-product-compliance
Lightning Source LLC
Chambersburg PA
CBHW020125170426
43199CB00009B/643